A STORM IN CAROLINA

THE SOMETIMES ODD, ALWAYS ENTERTAINING HISTORY OF PROFESSIONAL HOCKEY IN THE OLD NORTH STATE

JEB BOHN

Special thanks to:

Shawn Bednard
Paul Branecky
Ralph Slate

CONTENTS

AUTHOR'S NOTE

Growing up in North Carolina, hockey wasn't the first sport that typically came to mind. Baseball? Sure. Football? Of course. Hockey, however, wasn't something that I heard a lot about in my early childhood.

I spent a lot of time at my grandparents' house and they subscribed to several magazines (everything from Bon Appétit to National Geographic). Being the curious kid that I was, I would sift through them to see what I could learn about the world around me. This is how—at the age of 8—I first really started learning about hockey. The trigger? A cover featuring a man sitting behind an array of microphones, dabbing tears from his eyes.

The man was Wayne Gretzky.

I sat on the floor and read about his trade from the Edmonton Oilers to the Los Angeles Kings, a move that fundamentally altered the hockey landscape. At the time, I had no clue how significant this trade was, how it would spur the game's growth in non-traditional markets, and how interest in the sport would explode in the United States. Within a decade of this trade, the National Hockey League—through a combination of expansion and relocation—had teams placed markets like Dallas, Anaheim, San Jose, Miami, Tampa Bay, Phoenix, and Raleigh.

Of course, being in North Carolina when I first read the Gretzky article, I wasn't able to watch many games. During those early years, my greatest excitement came from watching ESPN's National Hockey Night. I waited each week for a game, eagerly anticipating the voices of Gary Thorne and Bill Clement. No, such sparse availability was not ideal, but it's what I had and I loved it. There was something about the game that spoke to me; I can't explain any better than that. There was just something special about it that drew me in.

As I got older, I developed a desire to play hockey in some significant way. My childhood best friend, Bryan, would come over and we would play on the walkway in front of my mom's house. The screen door—and a few panes of glass—suffered, but she didn't complain, at least not much. Soon after, our street hockey endeavor migrated to the parking lot of a church down the street. I had dedicated myself to the position of goaltender and spent hours skating around the lot in full gear, despite the heat and humidity of summer.

It was a lot of fun, though I drew some curious looks from passersby. I loved it, but I wanted to do more, so I joined the Parks and Recreation League in Raleigh. This was my first taste of organized hockey and, despite getting thrashed 8-2 in our first game, I was hooked. We played behind the Parker-Lincoln Building, in a parking lot, and I still have vivid memories of guys trudging down a small hill to retrieve roller hockey balls that sailed wide during warmups.

Good times.

The next chapter came one night, just before dinner. I sat in the living room reading the paper when I came across an article about roller hockey at a rink a half-hour from my house. I ate, threw my gear bag in the car, and went. Walking in, I expected to find a bunch of teenagers like myself. Instead, I found a mix of people my age and adults. There were guys from all over the US and Canada, most of whom had played at various levels throughout their lives.

One player was the facility's manager, meaning we could play for hours. It was challenging, and it was fun. Most of the guys bonded well and the few water breaks we took were littered with conversation and (mostly) good-natured chirping. Unfortunately, all good things must end. New management came in and, soon enough, they reduced our time. Soon after, I moved out of state. Save for the random game of floor hockey, that was it for my playing career.

That, however, is only a fraction of my love for the game.

Hockey—more than any other sport, I'd argue—is best viewed live; television coverage, even as much as it's improved, cannot do the game justice. The first game I took in was in the early 90s (I still have the ticket stub somewhere), seeing the Raleigh IceCaps at Dorton Arena. I went with my grandfather and, while he wasn't a huge hockey fan, he got into the spirit as soon as the puck dropped. It's one of my fondest hockey memories.

Once I got my license, I went to as many games as I could. Win or lose, I never had a bad time. Well, there was the night that my car—and several others—was broken into and vandalized, but that's a story for another day.

Of course, East Coast Hockey League games weren't the pinnacle of my fandom, but I'll save that for the book. Can't give away everything in a prologue, right?

The older I've gotten, the more interested I've become in the game's history. While that interest has always focused on the game as a whole, there's a special place for its history in my home state. I also love sharing information, hence the creation of this book. Regardless of whether you're a native North Carolinian, a transplant, or have never set foot in the state, I thank you for dedicating your time (and money) to reading this book.

There will be things many of you may already know, as well as tidbits you likely had no clue about. Bear with me, I'm writing this with everyone in mind. If you come across something you're already familiar with, enjoy reliving it.

Also, the end of this book includes season-by-season stats for each team, however, record keeping wasn't always detailed, so there are a few gaps. That said, I have done the best to gather as much information as possible.

With all of that out of the way, it's time to drop the puck!

CHAPTER ONE

Queen City Origins

CHARLOTTE REBELS (EHL; 1955-56)

AFTER A TURBULENT TWO-DECADE RUN, the Eastern Amateur Hockey League (EAHL) ceased operations prior to the 1953-54 season. After trimming their ranks from 28 teams to 22, the federation returned as the newly christened Eastern Hockey League (EHL) for the 1954-55 campaign. Following a four-year absence, the Baltimore Clippers returned to league play and, while their first season saw them tread water, there were a few bright spots for the Clippers.

Diminutive center Herve Lalonde racked up 22 goals and 50 assists in just 41 games. Winger Ralph DeLeo added 26 goals in 47 games while Al O'Hearn—better known as "Bibber"—picked up 41 points in only 25 games. There was youth and talent on the roster, leading to a need for patience. With the reborn franchise set to embark on their second season, there was reason for hope. Unfortunately, things would go sideways for the team.

Lalonde—the team's reining scoring champ—spent the 1955-56 season with Chicoutimi of the Quebec Hockey League (QHL). Their uneven play seemed to permeate their home rink as, on January 23, 1956, Carlin's Iceland caught fire and burned to the ground. With twelve home games remaining on the schedule, owner Charlie Rock faced a conundrum. Salvation appeared as a three-man faction spearheaded by Bill Shields.

Under the group's proposal, they would give the Clippers use of the newly opened Charlotte Coliseum. Able to accommodate 13,500 spectators for hockey, the Coliseum served as a desirable venue. Ultimately, the Clippers—under the Charlotte Rebels moniker—played six of their final twelve home dates in the Queen City. Playing their first game in the new venue on January 30, 1956, they dropped a 6-2 decision to the New Haven Blades. While the outcome was less than ideal, the Rebels drew a crowd of 10, 363 fans while approximately 3,000 had to be turned away.

That's a fairly impressive number for a new market with a vagabond team. Despite their continued subpar play, the Rebels drew an average of over 6,500 fans in each of the six games played there. Seeing the results at the turnstiles, Rock backpedaled on his earlier intent to return the team to Baltimore[1], instead opting to make the move to Charlotte permanent. Considering that their average attendance in their new home was triple that of their draw in Baltimore, it made sense from a business standpoint. The question became how it would pay off on the hockey side.

CHARLOTTE CLIPPERS (EHL; 1956-60)

Taking the ice as the Charlotte Clippers, the team came out hot to start the 1956-57 season. Over the course of 64 games, the Clippers lost just 13. Their offense proved too much for most opponents, led by 100 point performances from

O'Hearn (117 points), Doug Adam (114 points), Chuck Stuart (108 points), and Stan Werecki (103 points). Lalonde —back from his season in the QHL—added 97 points as Charlotte finished the season with a league-best 364 goals scored. The Clippers were the best regular season team— putting up a 21 game winning streak—before storming through the playoffs and capturing the Walker Cup as league champions.

Just like that, North Carolina had its first professional hockey title.

And it might not have happened. In November 1956, the Washington Lions made a hard pitch for Warecki. Rock stepped in and put an end to the attempt, but it stands to reason that—had they lost the skilled winger—their season may not have been as successful.

With Warecki safely in tow, the Clippers faced off against the Philadelphia Ramblers in a late-November contest. Tensions were high throughout the game, culminating in a scrum between Warecki and Philadelphia defenseman Al Fontana. Ken Murphy stepped in to defend Warecki, receiving a slash to the forehead for his trouble. As tempers reached a boiling point, Charlotte's John Brophy threw his stick into the stands following a scrap with Ed Bartoli.

With the game spiraling out of control, several Clippers accosted referee George McNeil to voice their displeasure. Coach Andy Brown eventually struck McNeil, resulting in police intervention. Through distraction or sheer anger, Charlotte lost focus and dropped the game by a score of 5-1. Thankfully, none of their players suffered any serious injuries.

The team also featured a young, standout defenseman by the name of John Muckler. The 22-year-old put up 52 points and 126 penalty minutes, acquitting himself as the Clippers' top defender. Muckler, however, is best remembered by hockey fans for the time he spent as a coach and general manager in the NHL. His greatest successes came with the Edmonton Oilers, where he won two Stanley Cups (1984, 1985) as an assistant coach, two more (1987, 1988) as the assistant head coach, and one (1990) as the team's head coach. He then had head coaching stints with the Buffalo Sabres and New York Rangers before spending six years as the general manager of the Ottawa Senators.

In net, responsibility fell to 22-year-old Les Binkley. The Owen Sound, Ontario native earned a spot on the EHL second All-Star team for his efforts in helping Charlotte to the top of the standings. Binkley is also a notable name as, during the NHL's first expansion, he signed with the Pittsburgh Penguins. He would play five seasons in the Steel City and return later as a scout. Binkley was serving in this capacity when the Penguins won back-to-back Stanley Cups in 1991 and 1992.

A newspaper article from December 1956 gave a detailed breakdown of the cost of Binkley's goaltending equipment:

- Belly pad: $20

- Shoulder pads: $10
- Sweater: $5
- Blocker: $20
- Catching glove: $20
- Pants: $25
- Skates: $65
- Goal stick: $5
- Socks: $5
- Goalie pads: $60

That's a grand total of $235 to outfit a goalie; not too bad. Of course, adjusted for today's dollar, that would be somewhere around $2400. Still, not awful (and my sympathies to those out there buying goaltending equipment for themselves or their kids).

For a relocated team in a new market, this was just about as good of a first season as anyone could hope for. While their second season saw the offense decline by 89 goals, the Clippers once again sat atop the league in 1957-58 and returned to the playoffs. Unfortunately, a distraction popped up when—during the postseason—word leaked that an ownership change was underway. Charlie Rock, who had moved the team to Charlotte, reached a handshake agreement[2] to sell his sixty percent interest in the team to Bill Allen and Jim Whittington. Completion of the deal would give the Charlotte duo full ownership of the team.

Despite this superficial accord, Rock didn't appear ready to part with the team. Over time, the deal morphed until they reached a final agreement, one that flipped the script of the original proposal. In the end, Rock purchased the shares of Allen and Whittington for a reported $20,000.[3]

This revelation sent shock waves through the team's roster. At a time when minor-league contracts held little guarantee, players were worried about their futures. Would there be salary cuts? Would the team release them outright? It was certainly an unwelcome set of concerns, especially for a team trying to repeat as league champions. The uncertainty led to seven players—with team captain O'Hearn serving as spokesman— to request their release from the team. While they deescalated the situation, there is no doubt that this had a negative effect on the team's focus.

The Clippers also had to overcome an injury to their starting goaltender when Binkley suffered a broken nose during their first-round series against the New Haven Blades. Ivan Walmsley—loaned to the team by the Philadelphia Ramblers—filled in admirably and led the team to a comeback victory in the series. Binkley returned for the championship round, though his level of play appeared to suffer when compared to his pre-injury performance.

"Let's face it, Les was never quite the same goalie. He wasn't as sharp and his reactions weren't as good. I don't think Washington would have scored the goals they did had Les

been the same tender he was the last week of the regular
season."
-Charlotte Clippers coach Andy Brown[4]

The final, and perhaps most insulting, intrusion came via winger Doug Adam, the team's leading scorer during the regular season. His coach noticed something distracted Adam as the playoffs got underway. Once the season was over, the answer became official: Adam defected, accepting a player-coach position with the Philadelphia Ramblers. They announced the move at a press conference featuring Adam and Ramblers' team president George Davis. Coach Brown didn't mince words when the topic of Adam's departure came up:

"I don't appreciate George Davis of Philadelphia talking with
him during the key moments of the season. Dougie was on the
phone constantly. I wish Dougie well in his new job, but the
offer came at the wrong time from a psychological standpoint."
-Charlotte Clippers coach Andy Brown[5]

Ultimately, they failed to defend their title, losing to the Washington Presidents in a seven game final series. In the wake of the ownership upheaval and uncertainty around the future, O'Hearn announced his retirement; veteran winger

Warecki followed suit. As training camp opened for the 1958-59 season opened in Hershey, Pennsylvania, both men reneged and joined the team. Mixed in with the familiar faces were a handful of new ones, reinforcements hoping to help return the Clippers to championship status.

Among the fresh faces was goaltender Denis Brodeur. Now, that name—or at least surname—will be familiar to pretty much everyone and for good reason. Denis' son is three-time Stanley Cup champion Martin Brodeur, holder of the NHL record for wins (691) and shutouts (125). While his son racked up a ton of accolades, Denis carved out a remarkable career of his own, capturing the Bronze medal with Team Canada in the 1956 Winter Olympics. After retiring as a player, he became the most iconic photographer in NHL while working as the team photographer of the Montreal Canadiens.

Brodeur's arrival was necessitated by the loss of Les Binkley, who departed for the Toledo Mercurys of the International Hockey League (IHL). With fresh blood between the pipes and peppered throughout the lineup, the Clippers opened the new season with high hopes. Those aspirations faded quickly as the team stumbled mightily and dropped in the standings like a stone through thin ice. By season's end, the Clippers sat dead last in the league, 27 points short of their total from the previous year.

Prior to the 1959-60 season, the EHL added two franchises—the New York Rovers and Greensboro Generals—bringing the league to eight teams. With new outposts in place, the league established two divisions, each comprising four teams. Clinton (NY), New Haven (CT), Philadelphia, and New York competed in the Northern Division; Johnstown (PA), Charlotte (NC), Greensboro (NC), and Washington battled in the Southern Division.

Once again, fresh faces came to camp, hoping to secure a spot. One notable attendee was Bobby Knievel, out of Butte, Montana. Knievel impressed the Clippers enough to earn a roster spot, though he eventually declined after deciding against playing on a team with such a travel-heavy schedule.[6] Instead, he returned to Montana and established the Butte Bombers before venturing into motocross and stunt riding. You may be more familiar with his stage name: Evel Knievel.

Along with the league, there were also changes for the Clippers. They let Andy Brown go, leaving a vacancy behind the bench. They filled the spot by hiring 35-year-old Pete Horeck as player-coach. The job in Charlotte was the first for Horeck, who had stints in Chicago, Detroit, and Boston over an eight year NHL career, brought a fresh perspective to the team. It worked as Charlotte finished second in their division and returned to the playoffs.

They drew their new intrastate rivals in Greensboro for the opening round, bowing out in three straight. It wasn't a return to dominance, but it *was* a step in the right direction. The next step was a change in ownership as Rock sold the team to the city with the caveat that Rock retained the rights to the name "Clippers." Once the transaction went through, the City of Charlotte held a contest, allowing fans to write in with suggestions for a new team moniker. Upon conclusion of the contest, the team selected NHL legend Maurice "Rocket" Richard to make the final decision.

His choice? The Charlotte Checkers.

CHARLOTTE CHECKERS (EHL; 1960-73)

Sadly, the new look and new name did nothing for the team's performance. The 1960-61 season saw the rebranded team finish at the bottom of their division and miss the playoffs. Muddying the situation was the fact that the City of Charlotte was losing money on the team. Attendance was down through the season, which cast a dark pall on the team's finances. The City was so eager to relinquish ownership that Coliseum Authority Chairman Arthur Newcombe suggested leasing the team for $1 per year.[7]

Local contractor Herbert Glenn attempted to purchase the Checkers, but he backed out in frustration in June 1961. A dedicated group of boosters—led by Al Manch—raised $30,000 and took over operations of the team for the 1961-62 season. While this left them with very little wiggle room, it ensured that the Checkers would stay in Charlotte for at least one more year. Unfortunately, the subsequent season saw a division-worst finish.

The team made minor improvements during the 1962-63 season, earning a third place finish and a berth in the EHL playoffs. The Checkers defeated the Knoxville Knights in the opening round before being eliminated in round two, once again at the hands of the Greensboro Generals. Looking to shake up the team, management brought in future NHL Hall-of-Fame goaltender Walter "Turk" Broda. Broda, winner of 302 games over 14 seasons with the Toronto Maple Leafs, got the Checkers back into the playoffs, though they suffered a first round sweep.

In case you were wondering who bested them, it was Greensboro. Again.

The Checkers made the playoffs consistently through the rest of the 1960s but failed to capture another championship. The 1970-71 squad proved to be a force, scoring more goals (383) than any other team in the league while also surrendering the fewest (153). Led up front by the lethal duo of Michel Rouleau (108 points) and John Gould (100 points), the punishing combination of Hal Willis and John Van Horlick on the blueline, and the steady play of goaltender John Voss, the Checkers set the league on fire. Apparently, it was a good year to be named John in Charlotte.

They continued their domination in the postseason, sweeping the Nashville Dixie Flyers in round one, putting up 29 goals in just four games. The second round brought another matchup against their rivals from Greensboro. This time, however, Charlotte came out on top thanks to a four-game sweep. The Checkers only managed 16 goals this series but ceded just three to the Generals. Having exorcized their demons, the hockey club from Charlotte earned a spot in the finals.

Their opponent for the championship series was the New Haven Blades, the top team in the Northern Division. While

New Haven's run through the playoffs had been every bit as impressive as Charlotte's, the team from Connecticut was out dueled in the end. The Checkers won the series four games to one and claimed their second championship and first since their inaugural season in the Queen City. A lot of credit goes to Fred Creighton, who had been the team's head coach since Broda's departure following the 1963-64 campaign. He spent years building his team, and it had finally paid off.

The Checkers blew out of the gates in the 1971-72 season, quickly showing themselves to be the best that the EHL had to offer. They finished again with the best record in both their division and the league. Their closest divisional foe—the Generals, naturally—finished with 22 fewer points than the Checkers. The closest team to challenge for the league lead—the Syracuse Blazers—had 16 fewer points. They were the cream of the crop and carried that confidence into the playoffs.

First up were the St. Petersburg Suns. Despite having a lackluster season, the Suns pushed the Checkers to six games before falling. For the second year in a row, Charlotte had reached the second round and, as many playoff series before, they went head-to-head with the Greensboro Generals. While they put up more of a fight than they had the year prior, Greensboro fell in five games. The Checkers were back in the finals, on the precipice of winning their second consecutive championship.

That's exactly what they did.

The boys from Charlotte executed their game to perfection, outscoring the second-place Syracuse squad 16-4 en route to a series sweep. Having spent so long in a fog of uncertainty, the team had pulled through and won back the hearts and pride of their city.

The good times, however, were short-lived.

Following the season, Creighton—who had served as the team's coach and general manager—resigned, moving to the same role with the Omaha Knights of the Central Hockey League (CHL). Creighton achieved a trifecta as the Knights won the CHL championship in his first season. In 1974, he became the coach of the NHL's Atlanta Flames, reaching the playoffs in four of his five seasons there. In 1979 Creighton was hired to coach the Boston Bruins but a contentious relationship with general manager Harry Sinden led to his firing before the end of the season.

Back in Charlotte, the Checkers hired Jack Wells to replace Creighton behind the bench for the 1972-73 season. Things got off to a rocky start as they tumbled down the standings, bumping their heads on every rung of the ladder. As the sun set on the season, the defending champs sat near the bottom of the league and out of the playoffs. The fall from grace was staggering and led to an offseason of change.

CHARLOTTE CHECKERS (SHL; 1973-77)

After the disastrous season, the team fired Wells and replaced him with Pat Kelly, who also took over general manager duties. The league itself underwent a major transformation prior to the 1973-74 season, effectively splitting into two separate federations. The Southern Division—home of the Checkers, Greensboro Generals, Roanoke Valley Rebels, and Suncoast Suns—became the Southern Hockey League (SHL). To augment the field, they added two expansion teams: the Macon Whoopees (no, I did *not* make that up) and the Winston-Salem Polar Twins.

This change, while creating stronger rivalries, did little to mask the financial issues that many teams (and the league itself) were facing. Cracks began showing when two teams (the Suncoast Suns and Macon Whoopees) folded before the first season concluded.

For their part, the Checkers had a strong season, picking up 44 wins and finishing second overall. The postseason brought yet another battle against the Greensboro General, a series in which the Checkers prevailed in six games. The next series pitted them against the Roanoke Valley Rebels, the league's best regular season team. Charlotte put up a fight until the end, ultimately falling in seven games. Their improved regular season performance and the emergence of winger Garry Swain provided reason for hope.

Prior to the 1974-75 season, the league added a new team. Originally slated to play in Fayetteville, North Carolina, they instead moved the franchise to Hampton, Virginia, giving birth to the Hampton Gulls. The Gulls, incidentally, were coached by former Charlotte Clipper John Brophy. The Checkers continued to improve, reaching the 50-win mark and the top spot in the league. They topped the season by capturing the James Crockett Cup as playoff champions.

With a relatively stable season under their belt, the league expanded once again, welcoming the Tidewater Sharks, who were based out of Norfolk, Virginia. As the 1975-76 campaign began, the Checkers regressed but only slightly, racking up 42 wins and securing the league's best record yet again. They bested Roanoke Valley in six games in the first round of the playoffs before defeating Hampton in five games to capture back-to-back Crockett Cups.

The league's tenuous financial situation reared its head again when Roanoke Valley folded ahead of the 1976-77 season. In spite of this, they added two new teams: the Baltimore Clippers (sound familiar?) and Richmond Wildcats. The reformed Clippers came over from the AHL while the Wildcats were an expansion team.

The Checkers regressed further, but their play soon took a backseat to the now insurmountable trouble that the league was in. By the time January 1977 was a week old, Greensboro, Richmond, Winston-Salem, and Norfolk had all folded. Initially, there was talk of adding a team to bring the league to four, but there was no money to do so. After several failed attempts to salvage the season, the league shut down, taking the Checkers with them.

This iteration of the team played their last game on January 30, 1977. In a poetic end fit for a movie, their opponent for this swan song was the Baltimore Clippers.

After coaching the premature end to the Checkers' final

season, Kelly became the head coach of the Birmingham Bulls of the World Hockey Association. He then coached the NHL's Colorado Rockies, beginning in the 1977-78 season. After reaching the playoffs in his first season behind the bench, Kelly's Rockies could not find their footing early in the 1978-79 season. As a result, they fired him 21 games into the campaign. This, however, wouldn't be the end of his hockey career.

In 1988, Kelly was one founder of the East Coast Hockey League and served as the league's commissioner for eight seasons. In 1996, the league changed the name of the playoff champions' trophy to the Patrick J. Kelly Cup.

CHARLOTTE CHECKERS (ECHL; 1993-2010)

Fifteen years after the dissolution of the SPL, a bid emerged to bring hockey back to Charlotte. A group comprising Felix Sabates—a Charlotte businessman—and Carl Scheer, president of Charlotte Professional Sports Teams Inc., were awarded an expansion team in the East Coast Hockey League (ECHL). As had occurred back in 1960, they held a contest to select a name for this new franchise and, just like before, this new team would be called the Charlotte Checkers. Sticking with tradition, the team would play in the old Coliseum, which was the focus of a $4 million renovation project[8]. Once completed, the building that played host to five championship teams became known as Independence Arena.

They brought additional investors on board, including

racing legend Richard Petty and his son, NASCAR driver Kyle Petty. As work was nearing completion on their refurbished home rink, the team itself was assembled. When it came time to select a coach, advice came from none other than Fred Creighton[9], the man who brought so much success to the city. His recommendation was John Marks, a former NHL defenseman who played in 657 games with the Chicago Blackhawks. In Marks, the Checkers got a coach who knew the intricacies of the game while possessing the tact to teach his players.

There was a lot of excitement about the return of hockey to Charlotte and the rebirth of the Checkers namesake. As the season approached, the city hosted an NHL exhibition game between the Boston Bruins and Philadelphia Flyers; the game was a sellout. To celebrate the home opener, singer Chubby Checker appeared to perform the national anthem and to provide entertainment during intermission. The enthusiasm that Charlotte had for hockey proved to be alive and well.

The team's first season saw them take the ice in the league's East Division, where they finished in fourth place. This earned them a playoff berth and a matchup against the Greensboro Monarchs. They bounced the Checkers from the postseason, but the new team now had a year under their belts. American center Matt Robbins paced the offense with 33 goals and 89 points; just behind him was Russian winger Sergei Berdnikov who tallied a whopping 48 goals and 87 points. Howie Rosenblatt brought a physical two-way game, notching 21 goals and 173 penalty minutes in just 44 games.

A blueline that featured smooth puck movers Derek Eberle and Joe Cleary complimented their well-rounded group of forwards physical, along with stay-at-home defenders Scott Meehan and Brian Blad. Most notable was Cleary's performance, netting 6 goals and 27 assists in only 34 games. The duo of Scott Bailey and Todd Hunter patrolled the crease, while Colorado-born Ken Weiss suited up for four games between the pipes. Also of note is that Brad Treliving—current GM of the NHL's Calgary Flames—appeared in six games on defense for the Checkers.

The goaltending lineup changed prior to the 1994-95 season; Bailey and Hunter were out, replaced by the tandem of Rob Tallas and Jon Hillebrandt. While other changes occurred throughout the lineup, it was again Robbins (28 goals, 89 points) and Berdnikov (37 goals, 74 points) who led the offense. Newcomer Shawn Wheeler put up 34 goals to go with his 226 penalty minutes. Dan Murphy led defenseman scoring with 4 goals and 37 points while Scott Meehan continued his reliable defensive play. Combined, their efforts were enough to earn a third place finish and a spot in the postseason.

It was another matchup against Greensboro and another first round exit for Charlotte. The team was trending in the right direction but needed to get over that playoff hump. As the team prepared for the 1995-96 season, several new faces were brought in, two of which stood out. One was goaltender Nick Vitucci, a veteran of seven seasons that included stints in the ECHL, AHL, and IHL. The other was center Darryl

Noren. Both players would end up making an enormous impact.

Vitucci brought stability to the crease in a way that the team had yet to see. They had received steady goaltending but relied on a regular rotation in each of their first two seasons. With Vitucci, the Checkers got a bona fide starter. Appearing in 48 games, the Welland, Ontario native picked up 32 wins. He gave the team a change to win every night and, as the season progressed, the team's confidence in their goalie grew.

Vitucci was also a creature of habit, sticking to a strict pregame ritual: pasta and a two-hour nap followed by coffee and stretching. Once on the ice, he would scrape up the slush from his crease, headbutt the goal (with his helmet on, of course), and slam against the boards. Goalies are a different breed, but it was impossible to argue against the results.

Noren was a familiar face, having played in 45 games with the Checkers in 1994-95 before being traded to the Monarchs. The Michigan native had been a solid performer throughout his career and 1995-96 proved to be a breakout season for him. The only Checker to appear in all 70 games, Noren led the team with 43 goals and 94 points. His point total set the high water mark for the young franchise, a record that would stand for five years.

In October 1995, female goaltender Manon Rheaume joined the team at training camp. Rheaume, who was not an official member of the Checkers, trained with the team as part of her preparation for the 1998 Olympics. While not under contract in Charlotte, she was available in case of emergency, though that never came to be. She appeared in one intra-team scrimmage, stopping 13 of the 15 shots she faced.

A one-week stretch from late December 1995, through early January 1996, saw a couple of impressive feats. On December 29, the Checkers entered a shootout against the Roanoke Express. Ultimately, Shawn Wheeler sealed a Charlotte victory; he was the 40th shooter of the contest. The following week, Vitucci stopped 54 shots in a 5-4 win over the Mobile Mysticks.

The team finished the year in 2nd place in the East Division and 3rd place in the league. They were heading to the playoffs yet again and seemed ready to overcome the demons that plagued them in years past. Once they got going, nothing was going to stop them. The Checkers went through Roanoke, South Carolina, and Tallahassee on their way to the championship round. Their opponent in the finals would be the Jacksonville Lizard Kings (you seriously cannot beat minor-league hockey team names).

The Checkers kept rolling, closing the series out in four games and capturing the Riley Cup. Vitucci's stellar play earned him the award for playoff MVP, a well-deserved accolade. Noren continued to produce, putting up 7 goals and 16 points. The real offensive star of this run, however, was Phil Berger. The veteran—who only suited up for 23 games during the regular season—exploded in the postseason, notching 10 goals and 27 points.

Also of note is that with this title, Vitucci had now won

the championship with four different teams, three of which were based in North Carolina:

- Carolina Thunderbirds (1989)
- Greensboro Monarchs (1990)
- Toledo Storm (1994)
- Charlotte Checkers (1996)

As the team prepared to defend their title, they looked for more players to step up their game. J. F. Aube, a right winger from Montreal, proved to be a standout offensive player. During the 1996-97 season—his second with the team—Aube dazzled on the ice, racking up 83 points to lead the team. Another Quebecer, David Brosseau, topped the team's goal scoring with 37. Despite some convincing performances, scoring dropped off significantly outside of the top six forwards.

On the blueline, the Checkers got a breakout performance from Mickey Elick. An eighth round pick of the New York Rangers in the 1992 NHL Entry Draft, Elick turned pro in 1996 after completing four years with the University of Wisconsin. The 22-year-old rearguard made a seamless transition, scoring 25 goals and 61 points. When injuries depleted the team's forward corps, the offensively gifted defender skated on the wing[10] in a game against Richmond on December 26, 1996.

Even with the ongoing injury concerns, the Checkers returned to the Kelly Cup Playoffs. They had the ill fortune of facing South Carolina, the league's regular season champions. The Stingrays stifled Charlotte and, with the exceptions of Brosseau and center Derek Crimin, neutralized the Checkers' attack. The absence of Aube, who suffered a concussion during the first game of the finals, didn't help Charlotte's chances. They were also without Noren, who had been called up to the IHL's San Antonio Dragons late in the season.

Just four days after the playoffs opened, the Checkers' title defense—along with their season—was over. It was a disappointing end to a campaign that started with much promise. Their beleaguered coach aptly summed up the series sweep:

"The whole difference was offense. We worked hard and played 2 1/2 good hockey games against a team that scored 71 more goals (during the regular season) than we did."
-Charlotte Checkers coach John Marks[11]

Eric Boulton appeared in 44 games with the Checkers during the 1996-97 season. The rugged winger would go on to play in 654 NHL games with the Buffalo Sabres, Atlanta Thrashers, and New York Islanders. On another note, the Checkers traded for young defenseman Jake Deadmarsh. While he never made it to the NHL, his older brother, Adam, had a nine-year career, most notably with the Colorado Avalanche with whom he won the 1996 Stanley Cup.

As is standard in minor-league hockey, the 1997-98 season

came bearing change. The ECHL realigned into a league of four divisions playing in two conferences. The Checkers found themselves in the Southeast Division of the Southern Conference. Aside from that, there were major changes in Charlotte's lineup. The team's three leading scorers from the previous year —Aube, Robbins, and Elick—departed in the offseason.

The Checkers still had reliable offensive players in Robbins and Brosseau and added a few players to help offset the losses. They brought in NHL veteran Mike Hartman for a combination of skill and leadership while 23-year-old winger P. C. Drouin sought to establish himself. A handful of future NHLers—Eric Boulton, Andre Roy, Dale Purinton, and Antti Laaksonen—also suited up for the team. Goaltender Nick Vitucci was also gone, leaving the duo of Paxton Schafer and Jeff Heil to handle the lion's share of the work. With the roster set, Marks' team got to work.

Noren, back from his call-up stint in the AHL, led Charlotte scorers with 74 points; Brosseau set the top mark for goals with 40. Drouin acquitted himself nicely, potting 21 goals and 67 points. The 30-year-old Hartman picked up 30 goals, though secondary scoring remained an issue. They played well enough to earn the sixth seed and dispatched Birmingham in the Conference Quarterfinals. That was as far as they would make it, as Pensacola knocked them out in the Conference Semifinals.

This season marked—no pun intended—the end of the road for Joe Marks in Charlotte. During the offseason, he signed a five-year deal to become both coach and general manager of the ECHL expansion Greenville (SC) Grrrowl. The change of scenery reunited Marks with former Checkers' co-owner Carl Scheer and allowed him to run a team in a much less crowded market. While the Checkers battled for attention with the NFL's Panthers and NBA's Hornets, the Grrrowl would be the only professional sports team in Greenville.

"We won't have to deal with the NBA and NFL. I feel like we've always had a very good product, but we've been on the back burner. I know Charlotte is a major-league town and we're minor-league but we've had a solid franchise and I'm a little disappointed in attendance last season."
-John Marks[12]

The team selected former Checker Shawn Wheeler to succeed Marks, giving the team a coach who was familiar with many of his players. J. F. Aube returned after a year away and finished first on the team with 82 points in the 1998-99 season. His 32 goals were one off of team leader David Brosseau while Darryl Noren—who also served as assistant coach—continued his consistent play. The veteran center ended the campaign with a 26 goal, 76 point effort. Offensive depth was again a concern, as was goaltending. By season's end, the Checkers had dressed six different netminders, most notably Taras Lendzyk.

The team struggled, ultimately missing the playoffs for the first time since their rebirth. The 1999-2000 season found the team regressing further, spiraling towards the bottom of their division. On January 13, 2000, with the Checkers carrying a record of 14-18-3, Wheeler was fired as coach and replaced by coaching veteran Don MacAdam. Sporting a head full of white hair and a thick mustache, MacAdam had been a head coach in the OHL and AHL along with a three-year stint with the Detroit Red Wings in the NHL. Prior to accepting the job, the 49-year-old MacAdam took in a couple of Checkers contests.

"I see every player in the lineup able to contribute more. I don't know any of the players. That's the toughest part. The players are the stars, they're what is going to make the team succeed."

-Charlotte Checkers head coach Don MacAdam[13]

Play improved little, and the team finished with a 20-43-7 record at season's end, outside of the playoff picture once again. Ownership had faith in their new coach and the belief that 2000-01 would yield better results.

It did, and one player addition did wonders for the team.

When he signed with the Checkers, Scott King had spent three seasons bouncing between the ECHL, AHL, and IHL. He had shown flashes of his talent, posting 72 points with the

ECHL's New Orleans Brass in the 1997-98 season. Perhaps there was something in the water in Charlotte; maybe it was divine intervention. Whatever the cause, King exploded in what would be his lone season with the Checkers, posting 40 goals and 101 points in 72 games. Second year Checker Kevin Hilton was next up with 19 goals and 80 points.

Eighth-year Checker Kurt Seher once again anchored a blueline that was bolstered by two-way defender Josh MacNevin. Wes Jarvis and Bob MacIsaac brought physicality to the backend, combining for 291 penalty minutes. The Checkers used five goalies during the season, but most of the workload fell to the tandem of Jason LaBarbera and Scott Bailey. Both tenders performed well enough to backstop Charlotte to a playoff berth. Their postseason presence was short-lived as the Dayton Bombers took the best-of-five opening round three games to two.

Looking to build on the previous year, the Checkers counted on a new forward duo. Dave Duerden, a 4th round draft pick of the Florida Panthers, came in and put up 31 goals and 78 points in what would be his last season of professional hockey. Brandon Dietrich—who spent 20 games with the Checkers the prior year—chipped in 29 goals and 74 points. LaBarbera started the year in Charlotte before moving up to the AHL and then NHL. Bryce Wandler and Scott Meyer carried the load, combining for 30 of the team's 41 wins.

The Checkers came into the playoffs on a high note only

to be eliminated in the first round again, this time at the hands of the Atlantic City Boardwalk Bullies.

Again, I have an irrational love of minor-league names.

This left the team with more questions than answers. Their level of play during the 2002-03 campaign was down, though only slightly. It was, however, enough to keep them out of the playoffs. The 2003-2004 season started on a more positive with the Checkers going on a 13-3-1 run early in the year. Inconsistency soon flared up again, sending the team into a slump that cost head coach Don MacAdam his job in late January 2004.

Team President Jeff Longo didn't have to go far to find a replacement, selecting former Checkers' goaltender Derek Wilkinson to take over as coach and general manager. The team responded by winning their first game under the new bench boss, but the shakeup wasn't enough to earn them a return to the postseason. For the second season in a row, there would be no playoff action in Charlotte.

This would be the last time that a Wilkinson-coached team failed to qualify for the postseason. Between 2004-05 and 2009-10, the Checkers averaged 38 wins per season, capped off with a 43-win, 94 point effort in the latter. This was good enough to claim the top spots in both their division and conference, though they eventually flamed out in the second round of the playoffs. Despite their consistent play, this iteration of the Checkers would not win another championship.

CHARLOTTE CHECKERS (AHL; 2010-PRESENT)

Another transition was in the works that would change the hockey landscape in Charlotte. Fortunately for the fans, there wouldn't be another 15-year gap as, in early 2010, Michael Kahn—owner of the Checkers since 2006—purchased the AHL's Albany River Rats and moved the team to Charlotte. The Checkers moniker was stripped from the ECHL team and transferred to the relocated franchise. The city relinquished its rights to the ECHL franchise, which reverted to the league.

The new AHL-based Checkers also carried over their NHL affiliation from Albany and served as the top farm team of the Carolina Hurricanes. Former Hurricanes forward Jeff Daniels remained as coach, a position he held for the team's final two seasons in Albany. His team gave the fans plenty to cheer about in their inaugural season, picking up 44 wins and fighting all the way to the Conference Finals. While many fans were upset that "their" Checkers were gone, this new version was began chipping away at any such resistance. This team featured a handful of players that would go on to play with the Hurricanes, most notably Justin Faulk, Riley Nash, Brett Bellemore, Zach Boychuk, Chris Terry, and Drayson Bowman.

The 2011-12 season proved to be a setback. Charlotte dropped 12 points in the standing and missed the playoffs. In net, Mike Murphy and future Hurricanes backup Justin Peters bore most of the starts. Twenty-three-year-old John Muse stole a significant amount of the limelight despite appearing in only

15 games. In those appearances, Muse posted a 10-3-2 record with a 1.81 goals against and a monstrous .941 save percentage.

NHL journeyman Dan Ellis joined the team for the 2012-13 season, appearing in 18 games while the NHL lockout raged on. A balanced attack helped the Checkers get back into the playoffs after a slow start, thanks in part to the play of the veteran netminder. The first round gave them a matchup against the Oklahoma City Barons, AHL affiliate of the Edmonton Oilers. The Checkers were able to push the Barons to the limit, but failed to win the deciding fifth game of the series.

The 2013-14 campaign was an interesting one, though not always in a positive way. Victor Rask—who would graduate to the Hurricanes the following year—began his first full professional season, netting 16 goals and 39 points. The Checkers also signed a pair of NHL veterans Manny Malhotra and Rick DiPietro to professional tryout contracts.

A strong defensive forward with some offensive pop, Malhotra first broke into the NHL with the New York Rangers during the 1999-2000 season. An errant puck struck Malhotra's left eye during the 2010-11 season, while he was with the Vancouver Canucks. He underwent two surgeries, missing the rest of the regular season before returning to the lineup in game two of the 2011 Stanley Cup Finals. Despite the successful surgeries, Malhotra suffered diminished vision in his left eye, a change that he worked to adapt to. The issue continued, leading to his removal from Vancouver's lineup just nine games into the 2012-13 season.

A free agent in the summer of 2013, Malhotra was determined to continue his career, but no NHL team made him an offer. A deal did eventually surface, as a 25-game tryout with the Checkers. While not an NHL deal, it gave him the chance to prove himself once again. Despite not registering a point through eight games, Malhotra showed that his prowess at the face-off dot and defensive acumen were intact. This led to the Hurricanes signing him to a one-year contract on October 31.

DiPietro represented another player whose career had been hampered by injury. The New York Islanders made history when they drafted the Lewiston, Maine native, first overall at the 2000 NHL Entry Draft, making him the first goaltender ever taken as the top pick. After struggling early in his career, DiPietro established himself as the Islanders' number one goalie and signed one of the league's more controversial contracts, a 15-year pact worth $67.5 million, in 2006. Unfortunately, the goaltender would soon earn the nickname "Rickety."

He suffered a series of concussions, interspersed with knee surgeries, groin injuries, hernia surgery, and an injured hip. No matter how hard he worked to get back into the lineup, DiPietro consistently found his way onto the injured reserve list. In the summer of 2013, less than halfway through his massive contract, the Islanders bought him out, making him an unrestricted free agent. His injury history scared teams away until the Checkers came knocking, tryout offer in hand.

With the season underway, DiPietro appeared in five games but could not find a comfortable rhythm; the team cut him in late November.

The Checkers would also host two goalies from the parent club, sent down separately on conditioning stints. First up was Anton Khudobin, recovering from an ankle injury suffered early in the season. The Russian goalie saw action in two games, posting a 1-1 record and earning first star of the game in his win after stopping 41 of 43 shots. He would return to the Hurricanes on New Year's Eve, 2013 but, within a month, the Hurricanes would send another goalie down.

Longtime Carolina starter Cam Ward—who had missed significant time battling injuries—was ready to return. In Raleigh, Justin Peters had been performing well and Khudobin was rounding back into form. To accommodate this, they sent Ward to Charlotte for a conditioning stint in late January 2014. He appeared in two games, posting a 1-1 record before being recalled by the Hurricanes. While these two events created some added spectacle, the Checkers still had to focus on winning hockey games.

Boychuk carried the offensive load, leading the team in goals (36) and points (74), followed closely by Terry's 68 points. However, the team could not keep the puck out of their own end—and, all too often, net—due in part to dressing nine goalies throughout the season. Muse got most of the starts and, while he put up good numbers, the team didn't have enough offense to keep pace with the league. They missed the playoffs for the second time in four seasons, an unsettling trend carried into the following year.

Looking for change, the team allowed Jeff Daniels' contract to expire, ending his run as Charlotte's head coach. His replacement would be Mark Morris, who had been head coach at Clarkson University—where he coached Hurricanes fan favorite Erik Cole—before moving to the AHL's Manchester Monarchs and then to the Florida Panthers as an assistant coach. Despite some improvement in their play, the Checkers missed out on the postseason for the third year in a row. After the season, Morris departed for St. Lawrence University, returning to the college coaching ranks.

NHL legend Ron Francis—then Carolina's general manager—turned to a familiar face and former teammate when he selected Ulf Samuelsson to take over Charlotte's coaching vacancy. A former NHL defenseman who played in over 1,000 games, Samuelsson held a handful of assistant coaching jobs in the AHL and NHL. The Checkers responded well to their new coach, gaining six points in the standings and earning a spot in the 2017 AHL playoffs. The Chicago Wolves ended Charlotte's season in the opening round and, as had happened the year before, they needed a new coach after Samuelsson left to accept an assistant coach position with the Chicago Blackhawks.

Enter Mike Vellucci.

A former minor-league defenseman—who saw two games of NHL action with Hartford in 1987-88—Vellucci had spent the prior 13 seasons coaching the OHL's Plymouth Whalers.

During his time in Plymouth, he accumulated 468 wins and on league championship, a pedigree that he looked to bring to Charlotte. Sure enough, his first season with the Checkers saw the team rise in the standings by 10 points. Center Lucas Wallmark led the team in points with 55 while Russian winger Valentin Zykov netted 33 goals for the top spot on both the team and the league. Roland McKeown and Trevor Carrick anchored the defense while the tandem of Alex Nedeljkovic and Jeremy Smith combined for 44 wins.

The playoffs saw a stronger, more focused Checkers squad take down the Wilkes-Barre/Scranton Penguins in a three-game sweep. The division finals series pitted them against the Lehigh Valley Phantoms, the second-best team during the regular season. Their domination continued and they dispatched the Checkers in five games but, more importantly, the young Charlotte team gained experience. As the 2018-19 loomed, they looked to build on that.

Headed by a forward group highlighted by Andrew Poturalski, Aleksi Saarela, and Martin Necas, the Checkers put up 255 goals, the second-highest total in the league and their third-highest since joining the AHL. Poturalski's 70 points placed him fifth in league scoring while a defense corps led by McKeown, Carrick, and an emerging Jake Bean helped tame opposing offenses while helping that of their team. Bean, in his first full season as a pro, scored 13 goals and 44 points; Carrick added 9 goals and 47 points.

In net, the Checkers leaned heavily on Nedeljkovic, utilizing him in 51 games. The 22-year-old Ohioan responded with 34 wins and four shutouts. He led all AHL goalies in wins, goals against average (2.26), and minutes played (2,917:19) while tying for the lead in shutouts (4). Because of Nedeljkovic's strong play—along with that of Dustin Tokarski, who enjoyed a 7-game unbeaten streak—the Checkers allowed only 189 goals on the year, the third-best mark in the league. The team had enjoyed an incredibly successful season, finishing with 110 points, the best total in the league and their best total since joining the AHL.

As the playoffs got underway, the Checkers made short work of Providence first and then Hershey, setting up for a conference final matchup against the Toronto Marlies. While Toronto had two of the top ten scorers—Jeremy Bracco and Chris Mueller—from the regular season, they could not contain Charlotte's attack and the Checkers claimed the series in six games, earning a berth in the Calder Cup Finals against the Chicago Wolves.

The series started off kilter for the Checkers who blew a two-goal lead in Game 1, ultimately losing the contest in overtime. Undaunted, they came out flying in Game 2, opening up a 3-1 lead before claiming a 5-3 victory and tying the series at one game apiece. Game 3 was much of the same as Julien Gauthier, Jake Bean, and Patrick Brown gave Charlotte a 3-0 lead after two periods. The teams traded goals in the third as Martin Necas picked up his fourth of the postseason. The Checkers won the game 4-1 and took a two games to one series lead.

Chicago pushed back in Game 4, carrying a 3-2 lead into

the third period. The Checkers needed a spark, and young power forward Nicolas Roy provided it with a game-tying-goal just 32 seconds into the final frame. Saarela potted the go-ahead-goal just over 12 minutes later and Roy added his second of the game into an empty net to close out the game. The Checkers were one win away from claiming Charlotte's sixth hockey championship and first since joining the AHL.

They didn't waste any time. Andrew Poturalski got Charlotte on the scoresheet just 91 seconds into Game 5. The teams spent the next two periods trading goals and the game looked to be over when Poturalski scored his second of the game into an empty net. Chicago didn't give up, drawing to within one after Cody Glass scored with 39 seconds remaining. In the end, Charlotte held on, bolstered by an insurance goal from Zach Nastasiuk. The clock ran out, and the Checkers celebrated as league champions.

On top of that, they also brought home some individual accolades:

- Alex Nedeljkovic - league's best goaltender
- Mike Vellucci - coach of the year
- Andrew Poturalski - playoff MVP

It was an unquestionably successful year, one that the team wouldn't get a chance to repeat. Vellucci left to take over the position of head coach for the Wilkes-Barre/Scranton Penguins. Ryan Warsofsky, who served as an assistant coach under Vellucci during the 18-19 season, became Charlotte's the new head coach two weeks later. With a new bench boss in place and an offense paced by Jake Bean, Steven Lorentz, Morgan Geekie, and Jaane Kuokkanen, the Checkers took to the ice to defend their title.

The team sat third in their division when, on March 12, 2020, the league paused the season because of the COVID-19 pandemic. On May 11, they officially cancelled the season, and no playoffs took place. The league prepared to return for an abbreviated 2020-21 season, though the Checkers were one of three teams electing not to take part.

CHAPTER TWO

Marching Into the Gate City

GREENSBORO GENERALS (EHL; 1959-73)

IN JANUARY 1958, ground broke on the Greensboro Coliseum Complex, a multi-venue complex designed both as a war memorial and as a way to raise the city's profile. Soon after the facility opened, the city began looking for a hockey team to play at the arena. The Eastern Hockey League granted them a franchise and a local group consisting of Carson Bain, John L. Randleman, and Sidney J. Stern, Jr., formed Central Carolina Sports, Inc. Their goal was to find a team to serve as the new EHL franchise. They soon found a match in the Troy Bruins, an Ohio-based team playing in the International Hockey League.

The group hired Rollie McLenahan, a former defenseman who coached the IHL's Cincinnati Mohawks to four consecutive championships, to coach the new team. He soon set about supplementing his roster to prepare them for the upcoming season. The first player signed was winger Don Carter, who had spent part of the previous season with Troy. The 23-year-old would go on to put up 18 goals and 69 points during the Generals' first season.

Remember that name, because it's going to be a constant.

The first season in Greensboro was bumpy, but the Generals made the playoffs despite finishing seven games below .500. There was talent throughout the lineup, with players such as Carter, Max Szturm, Frank Milne, and Chuck Holdaway emerging as standouts. A goaltender by the name of

Eddie Johnston started the season in Greensboro before being traded away to the Johnstown Jets. Johnston went on to enjoy a 17-year NHL career as a player before becoming a coach and general manager.

It's also worth noting another—albeit tenuous—connection that Johnston has to hockey in the state. On March 4, 1991, then-Hartford Whalers general manager Johnston traded franchise star Ron Francis to the Pittsburgh Penguins. This trade led to a downward turn for the franchise, one they never fully recovered from. Now, we all know what eventually happened there (and, if you don't, worry not—we'll get to it) so I won't get into the details here, though I wanted to mention it.

Back to the Generals.

McLenahan departed after the inaugural season, replaced by player-coach Ron Spong, a 9-year veteran of both the EHL and IHL. Brothers Bob and Bill Forhan were brought in to bolster the forward corps while Pat Kelly—the same Pat Kelly who went on to coach the Charlotte Checkers and help form the ECHL—brought a hard-nosed style of defense to the team. Don Campbell, a holdover from season one, handled the goaltending duties as the team embarked on a very successful 1960-61 campaign. Picking up 14 more wins than in their first season, the Generals finished tied for first in the league with the Johnstown Jets. Though the New Haven Blades—the top team from in the Northern Division—eliminated the Generals in the opening round, there were plenty of positives to take from the season.

Les Lilley, a skilled left wing from British Columbia, exploded for 52 goals and 111 points. Ron Muir—who would become a team fixture—scored 43 goals and 97 points in his first season with Greensboro. Spong did his part as a leader on and off the ice, notching 25 goals to go with 88 points. Kelly added 6 goals and 54 points from the blueline as well as accumulating 129 penalty minutes. The Generals had a strong core and looked to improve again in 1961-62.

Muir and Lilley continued their offensive dominance, racking up 100 and 95 points, respectively. Kelly continued his phenomenal two-way play, recording 4 goals and 69 points. Though they didn't perform better during the regular season, they won their division and earn a trip to the playoffs. They then dispatched the Clinton Comets and earned a berth in the finals, where they once again faced Johnstown, the defending champions. The Generals could not keep pace, falling in five games.

They had come up short but had also grown and gained valuable experience. They aimed to use this to make a leap forward and, boy, did they.

The Generals flew out of the gate once the 1962-63 season was underway, led by the dynamic line of center Don Davidson (22 goals, 103 points) flanked by wingers Gary Sharp (60 goals, 121 points) and Bob Boucher (60 goals, 107 points). Living up to his reputation as "The Bull On the Wing," Don Carter posted 90 points and 84 penalty minutes. The slick-skating Kelly continued to be a force on the blueline, notching 9 goals and 73 points. The offense put on a clinic night after night and the team finished with the league's top offense and didn't let up once the postseason was underway.

The Nashville Dixie Flyers were first up, cut down in three straight by the Greensboro juggernaut. Next up were the in-state rival Charlotte Checkers and, while they put up a fight, were unable to overcome the potent Generals' attack. The finals brought a clash with the Clinton Comets, who tied with the Generals for most points in the regular season. As the standings would suggest, it was a close series, one ultimately won by Greensboro. In the span of eight years, North Carolina had gone from zero hockey teams to two championships.

Things were good.

Davidson and Sharp carried the load again in 1963-64, putting up 120 and 108 points, respectively. Carter stepped up his game further, bringing his physical game to a new level. His hard work led to a 102 point campaign, complete with 111 penalty minutes. The Generals had another strong season, finishing second in the league and battling back to the Walker Cup Finals. Alas, a repeat was not in the cards; the Generals fell to Clinton in a five-game series.

In the 1964-65 season, the team was determined to return to championship status. The trio of Sharp (69 goals, 132 points), Carter (33 goals, 114 points), and Davidson (45 goals, 111 points) once again drove the offense. The team was hurt defensively when blueline fixture Pay Kelly's departed to become player/coach with the Jersey Devils. Rearguards Ron Quenville and Mike Kardash did their part, forming a duo that combined for 15 goals, 89 points, and 252 penalty minutes.

Goal scoring wasn't a problem; goals against were. The Generals surrendered 44 more goals than the year prior and their position in the standings suffered. These issues carried into the postseason, leaving Greensboro with a first-round exit and a long offseason. Compounding their struggles, Carter spent most of the postseason playing on an injured leg, which hindered his effectiveness.

"I hurt my leg that year, but I tried to play on it in the playoffs. They put so much Novocain in it that I don't think it thawed out until the summertime."

-Charlotte Checkers winger Don Carter[1]

The Generals suffered another loss when Davidson left to join the Clinton Comets prior to the 1965-66 season. Right winger Dom DiBerardino took it upon himself to pick up the slack, racking up 53 goals and 116 points while Sharp and Carter each broke the 100-point mark. Still, the team dropped to third in their division and sixth in the league, getting bounced by Charlotte in the opening round of the playoffs. 1966-67 was much of the same: a third-place finish and a loss to Charlotte in the first round.

Things picked up with the arrival of three 20-year-old forwards heading into the 1967-68. Bill Young, Bob Sicinski, and Stu Roberts all came in from the OHA's St. Catharines Black Hawks and became full-time Generals. More than that, the trio became key contributors:

- Bill Young: 37 goals; 59 assists; 96 points
- Bob Sicinski: 29 goals; 63 assists; 92 points
- Stu Roberts: 41 goals; 44 assists; 85 points

Not bad for three rookies.

The Generals rose in the standings, claiming the top spot in the Southern Division for the first time in four seasons. They ousted the Florida Rockets in the first round before once again clashing with Charlotte. The Checkers prevailed in six games before falling to the Clinton Comets in the finals. Despite losing to their rivals again, Greensboro was back on the right track.

The 1968-69 campaign marked the first time in nine years that Don Carter didn't suit up for the Generals after the veteran signed with the Denver Spurs of the WHL. Young defenseman Roger Wilson helped replace some of Carter's physicality while Sicinski broke the 100-point mark for the first time. Twenty-year-old Peter McDuffe carried the goaltending with a 36-19-9 record before being traded to Omaha of the CHL. The collective effort gave the Generals their second division title in as many years. Unfortunately, a series loss to the Dixie Flyers prevented them from reaching finals.

Greensboro was back with a vengeance in 1969-70, rolling over opponents en route to a 45-win season. Sicinski once again paced the team's offense, putting up 40 goals and 115 points while second-year center Moe L'Abbe led the team with 52 goals. Wilson continued his physical brand of defense, piling up 205 penalty minutes while also throwing in 13 goals. The Ontario-born due of Ernie Miller and Bob Smith manned the nets and the surging Generals marched back into the playoffs.

Greensboro outclassed the Jacksonville Rockets in the first round, outscoring their Floridian counterparts by a count of 35 to 8. The next round brought another skirmish with Charlotte and, while the Checkers put up a fight, it was the Generals who won the right to play for the Atlantic City Boardwalk Trophy. Their opponent was the Clinton Comets, the EHL's top regular season squad. The series was tight with each team fighting for every goal, every inch of ice. Ultimately, Clinton came out victorious, dealing the Generals a stinging blow after years of improvement.

With Sicinski moving on to the CHL's Dallas Black Hawks, winger Don Burgess (41 goals, 117 points) took over the title of offensive guru in 1970-71. Stu Roberts served as the team's most prolific sniper, picking up 62 goals while playing with a rough and tumble edge. The defensive pairing of Roger Wilson (21 goals, 70 points) and Ron Anderson (29 goals, 80 points) proved to be a force at both ends of the ice; Wilson also continued to make life miserable for opponents, accumulating an impressive 285 minutes in penalties.

Despite the offensive fireworks, the Generals weren't able to reclaim the division title, ceding to their I-85 rivals in Charlotte. As had become custom, the Generals clashed with the Checkers in the playoffs for a trip to the finals. Charlotte's high-powered attack proved too much to overcome, and they swept Greensboro on the way to winning the league championship.

Early 1971 marked a change in ownership when Central Carolina Sports sold the Generals to Carolina Cougars owner Tedd Munchak. A significant roster change came as well when the hard-hitting Wilson followed Sicinski to the CHL's Black Hawks. Newly acquired center Ron Hindson picked up the physical slack, spending 278 minutes in the penalty box, but the offense sagged. Greensboro finished the 1971-72 campaign with 56 fewer goals and 10 fewer wins that the year before but still managed a spot in the playoffs.

What came—naturally—was a second round matchup with the Checkers, who defeated the Generals on their way to a second consecutive championship. There was still talent in Greensboro, but the team wasn't seeing any progress. Prior to the 1972-73 campaign, Ronnie Spong was out as coach, replaced by Carter—who returned to the team during the 1970-71 season—in a player/coach role. The team responded positively before a blood disorder ended Carter's year prematurely. His successor as player/coach was goaltender Bob Smith.

GREENSBORO GENERALS (SHL; 1973-77)

The team's play showed improvement, but it wasn't enough to get past the first round of the playoffs. More change was on the way in the offseason, most notably the formation of the SHL. Coaching duties went to Ted Lanyon, a winger who spent parts of five seasons with the Generals. Things did not go well for the team in the new league, as they never posted a winning season. Over their final two seasons, the Generals won just 33 of 112 games.

An untenable financial situation led to the team moving from the Coliseum to the considerably smaller Piedmont Arena prior to the 1975-76 season. As the league itself struggled to remain solvent, teams began folding. The Generals lasted until January 4, 1977, when they officially ceased operations; the league itself shut down just four weeks later.

Despite the overall futility that the Generals experienced in the SHL, they featured some players who would go on to play in the NHL:

- **Kirk Bowman** (C): Bowman spent three seasons with the Chicago Blackhawks, appearing in 88 regular season and 7 playoff games.
- **Jeff Carlson** (RW): Carlson, who appeared in 21 games during the Generals' last season, never made it to the NHL. However, he has been immortalized in hockey history thanks to his role as Jeff Hanson, one of the exuberantly violent

Hanson Brothers, in the 1977 movie *Slap Shot*. His brother Steve Carlson—who appeared in the film as Steve Hanson—went on to appear in 69 games with the WHA's New England Whalers, a team we'll get to later.

- **Greg Fox** (D): Fox appeared in four games with the General during the 1976-77 season. He went on to enjoy an 8-year career spent with the Atlanta Flames, Chicago Blackhawks, and Pittsburgh Penguins.
- **Ed Johnstone** (RW): After putting up a very impressive 46 points in just 25 games with Greensboro during the 1974-75 season, Johnstone went on to a 10-year NHL career with the New York Rangers and Detroit Red Wings.
- **Michel Lachance** (D): Lachance suited up in 40 games for the Generals during their final season. He went on to appear in 21 games with the Colorado Rockies in the 1978-79 NHL season.
- **Barry Legge** (D): Legge patrolled Greensboro's blueline for 37 games in the 1974-75 season and later appeared in 107 NHL games with the Quebec Nordiques and Winnipeg Jets.
- **Steve Self** (RW): Self played in 65 games with the Generals over two seasons before making the NHL in the 3-game stint with the Washington Capitals.

GREENSBORO MONARCHS (ECHL; 1989-95)

Twelve years after the Generals last took the ice, Greensboro became the location of an ECHL expansion team. Dubbed the Greensboro Monarchs, the team entered the 1989-90 season under the guidance of head coach Jeff Brubaker. This was the first coaching job for Brubaker after retiring from a 12-year playing career that included 178 NHL games with the Hartford Whalers, Montreal Canadiens, Calgary Flames, Toronto Maple Leafs, Edmonton Oilers, New York Rangers, and Detroit Red Wings.

Their first season wasn't particularly impressive; the team finished 4th out of 8 teams and just two games above .500. They boasted three 30+ goal scorers (Phil Berger, Chris Robertson, and Boyd Sutton) but offensive depth was scarce. Still, the team qualified for the Riley Cup Playoffs and a first round series against the Virginia Lancers. Despite finishing 16 points behind the opponent during the regular season, the Monarch prevailed, winning the best-of-five series 3-1.

Their reward for this victory was a matchup against the top team in the regular season, the Erie Panthers. On top of finishing with 20 more points, the Panthers had scored 94 more goals than the Monarchs during the season. Regardless, Greensboro prevailed and earned a berth in the finals where they faced the Winston-Salem Thunderbirds. Once again, the Monarchs faced a top team and, once again, they prevailed, capturing the Riley Cup in their first season.

Much of the credit went to Monarchs' goaltender Wade

Flaherty, who earned the title of playoff MVP. This would be his only season with the Monarchs, as he moved on to the IHL and then the NHL. Over parts of 11 seasons, Flaherty appeared in 120 NHL games with the San Jose Sharks, New York Islanders, Tampa Bay Lightning, Florida Panthers, and Nashville Predators. Flaherty also holds the distinction of being the last NHL goalie to surrender a goal to Wayne Gretzky. After retiring, he moved on as a goaltending coach, first with the Chicago Blackhawks before moving to the Winnipeg Jets.

The 1990-91 season saw the team improve in all facets, led by center Len Soccio. The Thorold, Ontario native, led the team in goals (36), assists (55), and points (91); he also picked up 186 penalty minutes, good for fourth on the team. This team also featured a trio of future Checkers, with forwards Phil Berger and Darryl Noren along with goaltender Nick Vitucci all contributing to the team's advancement. The Monarchs powered through Cincinnati and Louisville before making a return trip to the finals. There, they faced the Hampton Roads Admirals, ultimately falling in five games.

Despite—or perhaps due to—failing to defend their championship, the Monarchs came into the 1991-92 campaign and stormed the league. Berger had a phenomenal season, posting 60 goals and 130 points to lead the team in both categories. His goal output was third-highest in the league and his point total made him the top scorer, finishing 11 points ahead of Dayton's Darren Colbourne. Burly winger Shawn Wheeler left his mark in a different way, amassing 301 penalty minutes. I should add that he did that in just 52 games and no, that is *not* a typo.

The team split goaltending duties between Vitucci and Greg Menges, and the tandem helped guide the Monarchs to a 43-17-2 record. They played well through the first two rounds of the playoffs, led by Berger's 21 points. The third round brought them a matchup against the defending champion Admirals, a series that Hampton Roads took three games to one. The Monarchs had their best season statistically, yet they had been unable to reclaim the championship.

The 1992-93 season marked a steep decline in the team's performance, dropping from 43 to 33 wins. They squeaked into the playoffs, edging Louisville out by a single point. Their postseason excursion, however, would be short-lived, as Erie eliminated them in the opening round. A series of mishaps had the Monarchs trending in the wrong direction.

This year's squad featured a young winger named Dan Bylsma who put up 25 goals and 60 points in 60 games. Bylsma went on to play nine seasons in the NHL, split between the Los Angeles Kings and Mighty Ducks of Anaheim. After hanging up the skates, Bylsma broke into coaching. His most notable post was with the Pittsburgh Penguins, serving as head coach for parts of six seasons, including a Stanley Cup championship in 2009.

The Monarchs bounced back in 1993-94, putting up a 41-21-2 record. Their offense took a major step up, thanks largely to a bounce back season from Berger. Leading the team in goals (56), assists (83), and points (139), Berger sparked a line that also featured Dan Gravelle (105 points) and John Young (104 points). Strong goaltending from the combination of Tom Newman and Patrick Labrecque helped steer the team to a first round victory over the Charlotte Checkers.

The second round brought another intrastate rivalry, this time against the Raleigh IceCaps. While it was a hard-fought series, the Monarchs came out on the short end, losing the series in five games. They had the talent, but could not get over the hump in the postseason and things weren't getting any easier. This applied to the team's home as much as their on-ice performance.

The Greensboro Coliseum was undergoing a $46 million renovation that had fallen well behind schedule. As a consequence, the city fired the contractor in charge of the refurbishment in May 1994. Off-duty members of Greensboro's fire department were hired to monitor events, a consequence of the fact that part of the uncompleted work included fire and safety equipment. Using the firefighters cost the coliseum $200,000 and, because of the tumult, Coliseum Manager Jim Evans resigned from his position.

Phil Berger, who had repeatedly proven himself as a potent offensive threat, split the season between Greensboro and the Detroit Falcons of the Colonial Hockey League. He did, however, put up 23 goals and 50 points in 40 games with the Monarchs in 1994-95. Winger Glenn Stewart and his 78 points picked up the slack from Berger's absence despite appearing in only 57 games. Still, the team struggled to a 31-28-0-9 record but made their way back to the postseason and all the way to the Riley Cup Finals before yielding to Richmond.

During their stint in the ECHL, the Monarchs set a league attendance record in a game against Charlotte on January 15, 1994. A crowd of 20,911 filled the coliseum and watched as the Monarchs dismantled the Checkers by a score of 7-1. The game not only set the attendance record, but beat the previous mark by just over 3,000 spectators. A rematch between the same two teams drew 16,377 fans on January 7, 1995, the fourth-highest attendance mark in ECHL history. This time Charlotte came out as victors in a 4-2 contest.

CAROLINA MONARCHS (AHL; 1995-97)

In early 1995, the AHL was seeking to expand, showing specific interest in southern teams who were a draw in their markets. This led them to invite five teams (Charleston, Charlotte, Greensboro, Hampton Roads, and Richmond) to make the jump from the ECHL. This came after an attempt to merge the two leagues was declined at an ECHL owners' meeting. Part of AHL Commissioner Dave Andrews' pitch to the five teams was that the league would waive its franchise fee —$1 million—provided at least four of the teams joined.

While the Monarchs' ownership group showed interest in committing to the move, the other teams were more cautious. Determined to move ahead, the team's owners reached a tentative agreement to purchase the Raleigh IceCaps and bring them along to the AHL. While the league was amenable to this, it didn't grant them the foothold they wanted. As a result, Greensboro would have to pay the franchise fee in order to join. They did so, but only after exercising the opt-out clause in their contract to buy the IceCaps.

The AHL officially approved the Monarchs' application to join in June 1995. Rebranded as the Carolina Monarchs, the team became the top farm club of the NHL's Florida Panthers. Rich Kromm, who played in the NHL for 10 seasons, became the team's head coach in July. It's important to note that this iteration of the team was a new and wholly separate entity from the ECHL team that came before. Prior to the 1995-96 ECHL seasons, the owners relinquished the old franchise to the league.

While the jump to the AHL meant a higher level of talent featuring players being groomed for the NHL, attendance lagged. During their six-year run in the ECHL, the Monarchs averaged just over 5,100 fans per game; in the AHL, that number fell to 4,400. The on-ice product didn't help lure in spectators either. In their 160 regular season games, the AHL Monarchs managed just 56 wins and failed to qualify for post-season play in either 1995-96 or 1996-97.

Then came May 6, 1997.

Peter Karmanos—owner of the NHL's Hartford Whalers—announced that he was relocating the team to North Carolina ahead of the 1997-98 season. Their ultimate destination would be Raleigh but, since their home arena wouldn't be ready until 1999, they needed a temporary home. Karmanos set his sights on the refurbished Greensboro Coliseum, though an agreement with the Monarchs' ownership would have to be reached. Aptly enough, Connecticut—the state that had just lost the Whalers—gained a new AHL franchise as the Monarchs moved there and became the Beast of New Haven.

While their time in the AHL was short, the Monarchs featured a handful of players who would go on to the NHL:

- **Bob Boughner** (D): The physical defenseman appeared in 46 games for the Monarchs during the 1995-96 season. He went on to enjoy a 10-year NHL career with the Buffalo Sabres, Nashville Predators, Pittsburgh Penguins, Calgary Flames, Carolina Hurricanes, and Colorado Avalanche. After retiring, Boughner went into coaching, eventually becoming a head coach with the Florida Panthers and San Jose Sharks.
- **Alain Nasreddine** (D): Nasreddine suited up in 89 games with the Monarchs between 1995-1997. While never becoming an NHL regular, he spent parts of 5 seasons in the league before transitioning into coaching. He then spent 5 years as an assistant coach with the New Jersey Devils before taking over as head coach during the 2019-20 season.
- **David Nemirovsky** (RW): A 4th round pick of the Florida Panthers in 1994, Nemirovsky appeared in 39 games over two seasons in Greensboro. He suited up in 91 NHL games, all with the Panthers.

- **Rhett Warrener** (D): Warrener only playing in 9 games for the Monarchs before making the jump to the NHL with the Panthers in 1995-96. He would play 12 seasons in the NHL with the Panthers, Buffalo Sabres, and Calgary Flames. Oddly enough, Warrener reached the Stanley Cup Finals on three occasions (once with each team he played for) but never captured a championship.
- **Kevin Weekes** (G): Weekes appeared in the net 111 times over two seasons in Greensboro, firmly establishing himself as the Monarchs' top goalie. He soon made the jump to the NHL, where he played for 11 seasons. During that span, he was a member of the Florida Panthers, Vancouver Canucks, New York Islanders, Tampa Bay Lightning, Carolina Hurricanes, New York Rangers, and New Jersey Devils. As a member of the Hurricanes, Weekes played an integral role in the team reaching the 2002 Stanley Cup Finals.
- **Steve Washburn** (C): A scoring machine in his time in Greensboro, Washburn put up 52 goals and 146 points in 138 games. He spent parts of 6 seasons in the NHL, putting up 29 points in 93 games with the Panthers, Vancouver Canucks, and Philadelphia Flyers.
- **Jason Podollan** (RW): Podollan scored 46 points in 39 games with the Monarchs in 1996-97 before breaking in with the Panthers. Appearing in 41

NHL games with Florida, Toronto, Los Angeles, and the New York Islanders, Podollan scored one goal and six points.

- **Ryan Johnson** (C): Johnson put up 18 goals and 42 points in 79 games with the Monarchs before making his NHL debut. He went on to appear in 701 games with the Panthers (two separate stints), Tampa Bay Lightning, St. Louis Blues, Vancouver Canucks, and Chicago Blackhawks.

- **Chris Armstrong** (D): After appearing in 144 games with the Monarchs, Armstrong bounced around the minors for a few seasons before breaking in with the Minnesota Wild during the 2000-2001 campaign. He would appear in a total of seven games with the Wild and the Mighty Ducks of Anaheim.

- **Herbert Vasiljevs** (RW): The Latvian winger played in 54 games in Greensboro in 1996-97. His first NHL action came with the Panthers two years later followed by stints with the Atlanta Thrashers and Vancouver Canucks. In 51 NHL games, Vasiljevs scored eight goals and 15 points.

- **Filip Kuba** (D): The big defender appeared in 51 games with the Monarchs in 1996-97. Two years later, he transitioned into the NHL with the Panthers. He went on to have a 14-year career, appearing in 836 games with the Panthers,

Minnesota Wild, Tampa Bay Lightning, and Ottawa Senators.

GREENSBORO GENERALS (ECHL; 1999-2004)

As the Hurricanes prepared to move east to their new arena, plans were underway to bring minor-league hockey back to Greensboro. A local group headed by attorneys Art Donaldson and James Roscetti lobbied to bring in an ECHL team to play in the Coliseum. In July 1999, they were granted a franchise and adopted the handle of the city's first team, the Greensboro Generals. They hired former Monarchs' coach Jeff Brubaker to lead the new team.

Their first two seasons did little to establish the new generation of Generals as a force in the league. A 20-win campaign in 1999-2000 was followed by 26 wins the season after. A coaching change prior to the 2001-2002 season did little to correct their course, and they finished in the league's basement. Another coaching change took place before the 2002-2003 season, with Rick Adduono taking over behind the bench. Adduono—who led the South Carolina Stingrays to a Kelly Cup championship in 2001—came in and got immediate results.

Under their new coach's guidance, the Generals won 42 games and finished second in their division. Mark Turner, a 12-year veteran of various minor leagues, led the team with 63 points. Sam Ftorek—son of 8-year NHL veteran Robbie Ftorek—served as an offensive and physical force, putting up

61 points and 135 penalty minutes from the blueline. The Generals also found stability in net with goaltender Daniel Berthiaume. A nine-year NHL vet, Berthiaume racked up a 30-14-5 record in his first season in Greensboro.

The Generals earned their first playoff appearance, facing the Roanoke Express in the divisional semifinals. Greensboro came out firing, taking the first game by a score of 7-2 and winning the series three games to one. The second round opponent was the Atlantic City Boardwalk Bullies. The play was tight with each of the first two games going into overtime. Atlantic City prevailed, eliminating the Generals in four on their way to a Kelly Cup championship.

The 2003-04 season was a setback for the team, off the ice as well as on. The Generals dropped 11 points in the standings and missed the postseason for the fourth time in five seasons. This, however, was far from the only issue facing the franchise. There were many things brewing behind the scenes that ultimately led to the team's demise.

In 2001, former coach Jeff Brubaker sued the team for wrongful termination and the unpaid salary that was due for the final year of his contract, amounting to $109,752.[2] In 2003 Brubaker was awarded a judgment in his favor however, the legal spat continued. We'll come back to that in a moment.

The team was in financial trouble and, in 2003, owner Art Donaldson sought to unload the team. Not wanting to continue ownership of a depreciating asset, Donaldson reached an agreement to lease the team to a pair of local businessmen. These interim owners immediately stated that they needed one year to put an adequate ownership group together. During this time, the City of Greensboro took control of the team for the duration of the 2003-04 season. This brought a new wrinkle to the lawsuit when Brubaker's lawyer added the city to the list of defendants in his case.

By the end of the season, and with no new ownership group formed, the city rescinded their controlling interest in the team. Following these developments, the league dissolved the franchise. Other attempts were made to secure stable ownership for the Generals, but none came to fruition. After five short years, the second incarnation of the team faded into memory.

CHAPTER THREE
Party of Nine in the Twin City

FOR ANYONE not from the area, it may come as a surprise that the busiest hockey city in North Carolina (at least in terms of quantity) is Winston-Salem. While they were later to the party than their Piedmont brethren in Charlotte and Greensboro, the city has embraced the sport for almost 50 years.

WINSTON-SALEM POLAR TWINS (SHL; 1973-77)

When the Southern Hockey League formed in 1973, they needed teams to round out their ranks. To do this, the new league brought in two expansion teams; one in Macon, Georgia, and the other in Winston-Salem. The team was owned by a group of 15 investors and would make their home in the Winston-Salem Memorial Coliseum. When it came time to select a coach, the team had only to look 30 miles east.

Don Carter had established himself as a legend in Greensboro, thanks to spending 12 years there as a player and a coach. Carter brought a winning pedigree and a knack for leadership to the fledgling franchise. Management assembled the team's roster and the Polar Twins embarked on the 1973-74 SHL season. There were bright spots, notably the performance of Howie Colborne. The prickly winger scored 33 goals and 81 points in the team's inaugural season. That's particularly impressive, considering he also spent 131 minutes in the penalty box.

The team boasted two other 30-goal scorers in Brian Carlin (36) and Bernie Blanchette, who led the team with 39.

Defense proved to be much harder, and they finished with the most goals allowed (363) in the league. Following a disappointing season, Carter was ousted as coach and replaced by Forbes Kennedy. Kennedy, a former player who appeared in 603 NHL games, looked to turn around the team's fortunes. If they were going to be successful, they would have to do it without their top five scorers from the year before.

The 1974-75 season saw 19-year-old rookie Ken Gassoff step in and lead the team in scoring with 86 points. Defensemen Blaine Rydman and Ron Fogal gave the fans plenty to cheer for as well, piling up 444 penalty minutes between them. The team improved on their first season, raising their goals for by 17 while reducing their goals against by 18. They finished one position higher in the standings, though that was the extent of their success.

1975-76 brought more improvements to the team's performance. John Campbell, in his second year with the team, racked up 33 goals and 92 points. Gassoff remained an integral part of the offense, pacing the team with 36 goals. They picked up nine points in the standings, but remained firmly entrenched in third place. Staying the course, the Polar Twins suffered an early playoff exit to cap off the season.

In January 1976, with the team struggling to find a consistent effort, the team released general manager Bob Smith. Jim Crockett, Jr., who purchased the team a month prior, recruited former Charlotte Clippers/Checkers defenseman Gordie Tottle to fill the role. Through the course of the year, Tottle would move from that position to director of player personnel before being named coach in November. The job with the Polar Twins wasn't Tottle's only job; it wasn't even his primary post. The retired defender had spent a decade as the owner-operator of a service station in Charlotte.

It was normal for the coach to spend a full day changing oil and patching tires before meeting up with the team prior to a game. While it was clear that he still loved the game and enjoyed coaching, becoming a full-time coach was not an endeavor that held much sway with Tottle.

"I don't want to coach full-time. I want to continue my business here. If I leave it and coach full-time, I could be out of a job anytime, especially with the way this league is."
-Polar Twins coach Gordie Tottle[1]

Tottle's words would prove prophetic in short order. There were rumblings throughout the league of financially unstable teams on the verge of collapse. Then, in the first week of January, 1977, the bottom fell out when the Polar Twins— along with three other teams—ceased operations. The league attempted to carry on, either through a tournament to determine a league champion or a partnership agreement with another league. Both the International Hockey League and the North American Hockey League rejected these proposals and, on January 31, 1977, the SHL shut down.

CAROLINA THUNDERBIRDS (ACHL; 1981-87)

In 1981, a new league rose from the ashes of the second iteration of the Eastern Hockey League. Dubbed the Atlantic
Coast Hockey League (ACHL), the federation consisted of
seven teams. The roster included a new franchise in the Twin
City, christened the Winston-Salem Thunderbirds, who would
play in the Memorial Coliseum. The team brought Curry
Whittaker on board to coach the squad for what would be a
very inauspicious 1981-82 season.

The team struggled mightily, mustering just 14 wins
during their 50-game campaign. Forward Peter Dunkley
managed 24 goals and 50 points, leading the Thunderbirds in
both categories. There were, however, plenty of issues. Instability hindered the team's fortunes in net, and they would
dress nine different goaltenders through the course of the
season. Their on-ice performance did little to help their attendance, and the team routinely drew less than 2,000 fans per
game. As a result, the burgeoning franchise found itself on
shaky financial ground.

In an effort to keep the team afloat, owner Dave Gusky
reached out to recently retired NHL player Rick Dudley for
guidance in February of 1982. Dudley agreed to consult and
quickly realized how close the Thunderbirds were to founder-
ing. With Gusky seeking to cut ties and sell the team, Dudley
agreed to help find a buyer to take over. When the search
failed to yield results, Dudley purchased the team himself and
began selling stock for $10 per share.[2] He made every effort to

improve the team's standing, both in the league and in the community.

As part of his agreement to purchase the Thunderbirds, Dudley covered a significant amount of debt that the previous ownership regime accumulated. More than once, he found himself writing personal checks to cover the team's payroll. Not eager to bankrupt himself, Dudley attempted to save money wherever he could. Part of this included acting as the team's bus driver and undertaking any task he could handle himself. Anything that could reasonably (and unreasonably) be asked of an owner, Dudley did.

And then some.

Ahead of the 1982-83 season, Dudley replaced Whittaker behind the bench and took on the duty of the general manager. His first order of business was revamping the name, rebranding the team as the Carolina Thunderbirds hoping to draw from a wider base of potential fans. Next up was adding talent to the lineup, and Dudley's years in the NHL provided him with ample connections to do so. New additions Brian Carroll and Michel Lanouette became major contributors offensively and helped the Thunderbirds double their goal output from the year before.

The biggest star to emerge on the team was Dave Watson, a 24-year-old forward who had two short stints with the NHL's Colorado Rockies. Appearing in 66 games for Carolina, Watson scored 53 goals and 102 points. Under Dudley, the team played a physical brand of hockey, rolling over opponents with a barrage of goals and hits. While there was still instability in goal—the team dressed seven different goalies during the 82-83 campaign—team defense improved and the Thunderbirds finished the season with a 51-10-7 record, good enough to make them the league's top team in the regular season.

To put just how good their performance was into perspective, the second-place Erie Golden Blades finished with 28 fewer points than the Thunderbirds. The opening round of the playoffs saw Carolina sweep the Virginia Raiders in four games, outscoring their opponent by a margin of 28-6. With a berth in the finals, they met up with the Mohawk Valley Stars and again the Thunderbirds dominated. The result was another sweep, this time to the tune of a 21-9 goal differential. The turnaround the team had seen under Dudley was staggering.

The Thunderbirds hit the ice for the 1983-84 season with the goal of defending their title. Second-year center Kim Elliot had a breakout performance, putting up 48 goals and 124 points. He was joined in the century club by Benoit Laporte and Brian Carroll, who both finished the season with 102 points. The goaltending platoon finally settled down as well, with the duo of Pierre Hamel and Paul Skidmore handling the majority of duty. Hamel—a veteran of 69 NHL appearances with Toronto and Winnipeg—led the way with 25 wins and two shutouts.

The playoffs brought another first round matchup against Mohawk Valley and, while not as dominant as the year before, Carolina prevailed in five games. Erie, who finished just one point back during the season, became the last obstacle to the Thunderbirds repeating as champions. In the end, Carolina couldn't overcome their opponent, as Erie controlled the series and claimed victory in five games. It may have been disheartening, but it did nothing to derail what Dudley had built.

The 1984-85 team came flying out of the gates and up the standings. Then again, that was becoming old hat for the Thunderbirds. Elliot set the offensive bar again with a 30 goal, 97 point effort; Lanouette finished just behind with 37 goals and 93 points. Rookie John Torchetti made an impressive debut, leading the team with 44 goals; fellow neophyte Ed Christian was right behind him with 43. Hamel teamed with Dan Olson to provide a reliable tandem in goal, combining for a 53-10-0-1 record. Season's end saw Winston-Salem again at the top of the league with 107 points, 24 ahead of their closest competitor.

Hamel took over starting duties as the playoffs started and Carroll elevated his play following a setback in his play during the season. The Lancers of Virginia once again found themselves in the way of a steamroller Thunderbirds team, dropping four straight while Carolina outscored them 41-16. The final series brought a rematch with Erie, again with the title on the line. This time, however, the Thunderbirds wouldn't be denied and, after a hard-fought six-game series, they reclaimed their status as league champions.

1985-86 brought another breakout campaign, this time from second-year center Joe Curran. The University of Massachusetts Boston alum tallied 42 goals and 124 points in 61 games. His performance was impressive enough to earn him the title of ACHL MVP for the season. The roster also featured two 50-goals scorers in Torchetti (51) and rookie Andy Cozzi (52). The Thunderbirds also received a standout performance in net from 20-year-old Ray LeBlanc.

LeBlanc—who would go on to earn acclaim as the US team's goaltender at the 1992 Winter Olympics—posted a 33-9-0 record with three shutouts. Between his solid goaltending and the offense exploding for 397 goals on the year, the Thunderbirds again found themselves at the top of the standings. Curran kept his pace up in the playoffs, picking up 12 goals and 19 points as Carolina earned a third consecutive finals matchup against the Erie Golden Blades. The Thunderbirds dictated the play and took the series in five games, winning their third championship in four years.

A notable change took place following the win as Dudley —who had sold his interest in the team—departed to accept a coaching position in the IHL. Mark Huglen, a former Thunderbirds player, assumed head coaching duties for the 1986-87 season. The team responded poorly, enduring an 11-game losing streak before former goaltender Pierre Hamel replaced Huglen in January 1987. The change did little to change the team's fortunes, and they finished in fourth place before being eliminated from the playoffs by the Virginia Lancers. It's also worth noting that the coach of this Virginia team was John Tortorella, who would go on to a very successful career as a coach in the NHL.

Despite the drastic drop in performance, there were still

positives to take away for the Thunderbirds. Second-year center Doug McCarthy led the league in assists (73) and points (110) while Scott Knutson (33 goals, 91 points) was named Rookie of the Year. While these two provided bright spots, the team was in dire need of a fresh start. Issues with the league would soon give them an opportunity to do so.

CAROLINA THUNDERBIRDS (AAHL; 1987-88)

By the summer of 1987, ACHL membership had dwindled to three teams. On June 24, 1987, the league announced that operations for the 1987-88 would be indefinitely suspended; the Thunderbirds—along with the Virginia Lancers—joined the All-American Hockey League (AAHL) while the Erie Golden Blades shut down operations. As is often the case with minor-leagues, especially at the time, the AAHL was not the most stable environment. Regardless, the Thunderbirds took advantage of their situation and made the best of it.

Led by John Torchetti's 134 points—including 63 goals— the Thunderbirds scored a league-leading 355 goals. Diminutive forward Steve Plaskon put up 106 points and 223 penalty minutes, leading the team in the latter category by a wide margin. Their performance was enough to carry the team to a second-place finish, though they saved their best for the play-offs. It might have been a new league, but the finals once again came down to Carolina butting heads with Virginia. Unlike the year before, the Thunderbirds would emerge victorious.

CAROLINA/WINSTON-SALEM THUNDERBIRDS (ECHL; 1988-92)

Following their lone season in the AAHL, the Thunderbirds left to become one of the founding members of the East Coast Hockey League. During their first season in the new league, the Thunderbirds posted an unimpressive 27-32-0-1 record. Perhaps the most notable statistics about the 1988-89 season were that the team went through four coaches and dressed eight goaltenders. To say there was upheaval would be an understatement, though the team still earned a spot in the postseason. More than that, they won their way into the finals before capturing the league's first championship.

Prior to the 1989-90 season, the team reverted to calling themselves the Winston-Salem Thunderbirds. The name change worked, and the team posted a 38-16-0-6 record and finished in a tie for the league's top spot. Not content, they worked their way back to the Riley Cup Finals, facing off against the Greensboro Monarchs. The Monarchs gained an early edge in the series and didn't relent, eliminating the Thunderbirds in five games. Though they failed to win back-to-back titles, you could hardly consider Winston-Salem's first two seasons in the ECHL anything other than successful.

The 1990-91 season was a completely different story.

The Thunderbirds stumbled out of the gate, digging themselves into a hole they could not climb out of. As the season came to an end, they sat in the league's basement with a record of 20-41-0-3, 16 points below the second-worst team. Their goal output was second-lowest in the league while their goals allowed ranked dead last. It was a season to forget.

The team named Doug Sauter as head coach prior to the 1991-92 season, the fourth person to hold that position in the three seasons they existed in the ECHL. The Thunderbirds improved, gaining 33 points in the standings and returning to the playoffs. Their run was short-lived, however, as they bowed out in the first round to the Richmond Renegades. While it was a big step towards correcting their course, the fans in Winston-Salem wouldn't get a chance to see what came next. Following the end of the season, an announcement came stating that the Thunderbirds would relocate to Wheeling, West Virginia, prior to the 1992-93 season.

WINSTON-SALEM MAMMOTHS (SHL; 1995-96)

The summer of 1995 saw the formation of a new version of the Southern Hockey League (SHL), a minor league which originated in Florida. Six teams comprised the league, including an entry from Winston-Salem known as the Mammoths. Coaching duties went to former NHL player John Anderson, a veteran of 12 seasons. The offense was led by Yvan Corbin (95 points) and Alexei Deev (88 points) while the defensive side was anchored by Alain Cote, Hayden O'Rear, and goaltender Wayne Marion.

The Mammoths finished third in the league, good enough to see playoff action. Corbin again carried the offensive load, racking up a mind-boggling 14 goals and 30 points in 9 postseason games. Winston-Salem made short work of the Daytona Beach Breakers in the opening round before falling to the Huntsville Channel Cats in a five-game championship series. Unfortunately, that would be all she wrote for the Mammoths; the league did not play another season and four of its teams (*not* including the Mammoths) moved into the Central Hockey League.

WINSTON-SALEM ICEHAWKS (UHL; 1997-99)

In another strange tale of minor-league hockey, we look to the Utica Blizzard of the Colonial Hockey League. After three years of playing in the Mohawk Valley, the team could not reach a mutually beneficial lease agreement with their home rink. In a move reminiscent of the Baltimore Clippers coming to Charlotte, owner Jeff Croop relocated the Blizzard to central North Carolina. Operating as the Winston-Salem IceHawks, the franchise also changed leagues, becoming a member of the United Hockey League. On top of that, the team got a new coach (former NHLer Robert Dirk) and several new players.

The 1997-98 season did not go smoothly for the transplanted team, as they scored just 228 goals, the lowest total in the league. The lone player to break the 30-goal mark was winger Darren Schwartz, who finished the campaign with 42. Mark Richards and Bill Horn split most of the goaltending duties, the pair accounting for 28 of the team's 33 wins. Unfortunately, the IceHawks finished fourth in their division, outside of the playoffs. Following the season, the team changed coaches, replacing Dirk with Mike Sauter.

The team actually took a small step back in the 1998-99 season, finishing with fewer points than the year prior. Luckily, divisional realignment ensured the IceHawks would see post-season action. Former Mammoth Alexei Deev led the team in points (84), barely edging out winger Jeffrey Azar (83). Their regression showed in the playoffs as the Muskegon Fury thoroughly outpaced them in the first round. The IceHawks dropped four straight after winning game one, giving the season a disappointing end. Afterward, the team returned to New York State, settling in Glenn Falls under the Adirondack IceHawks moniker.

WINSTON-SALEM PARROTS (ACHL; 2002-03)

In yet another weird situation, we move down to St. Petersburg, Florida, home of the Parrots. People were slow to take to the team and attendance suffered badly, with an average of under 800 fans per game. Worst of all was their second home game of the 2002-03 season, attended by a paltry 189 spectators.[3] The team's owner, along with Atlantic Coast Hockey League officials, began looking for a suitable home for the Parrots, ultimately deciding on Winston-Salem.

The team struggled in their new home, both on the ice and in the stands. Head coach Bruce Ramsay was fired during the season and replaced by Darryl Noren, a former member of the Greensboro Generals and Charlotte Checkers. The change behind the bench did little to improve the team's play; the Parrots finished the year with a record of 28-23-6. Despite their lackluster play, they managed to secure the final playoff spot and a first round matchup with the Knoxville Ice Bears. The Parrots struggled, netting just one goal as Knoxville swept them in three games.

Attendance didn't improve during their stint in the Twin City, exacerbating the team's dire financial situation. With their current outlook being unfavorable, the league felt that the best option would be to fold the team as opposed to another costly move. Just like that, the strange saga of the St. Pete/Winston-Salem Parrots was over.

WINSTON-SALEM T-BIRDS (SEHL; 2003-04)

The summer of 2003 marked the birth of the South East Hockey League (SEHL). One of the smallest minor leagues, the SEHL embarked on its debut season with four teams:

- Cape Fear Fire Antz
- Huntsville Channel Cats
- Knoxville Ice Bears
- Winston-Salem T-Birds

There was originally supposed to be a fifth team—the Tupelo T-Rex—but a conflict with the CHL prevented them from joining. With the four squads set, the SEHL began a 56-game 2003-04 season. To say that things did not go smoothly for the T-Birds is an understatement. An anemic offense left them unable to compete with their league brethren. On top of their on-ice struggles, the team had trouble drawing fans, averaging fewer than 800 patrons per game.

These issues culminated at season's end when the T-Birds —along with Huntsville—folded. Following these events, the league itself shut down operations.

WINSTON-SALEM POLAR TWINS (SPHL; 2004-05)

The failures of a handful of other minor-leagues—The Atlantic Coast Hockey League, the South East Hockey League, and the World Hockey Association 2—led to the creation of the Southern Professional Hockey League in 2004. The federation set up to play a 56-game season for 2004-05 with eight teams, including three in North Carolina (Asheville, Fayetteville, Winston-Salem). Assuming head coaching duties for the Winston-Salem franchise was Bryan Wells, a former member of the Carolina Thunderbirds.

The second-generation Polar Twins took the ice to mostly poor results. Losing streaks added up until the end of the campaign as the team struggled at both ends of the ice. Finishing with a league-worst 14-42 record, the Polar Twins scored the fewest goals in the SPHL (174) while allowing the most goals against (300). There were no playoffs and—soon after—there were no Polar Twins. While they drew better attendance that the Parrots or T-Birds, it wasn't enough and the team folded after their inaugural season.

TWIN CITY CYCLONES (SPHL; 2007-09)

The Southern Professional Hockey League welcomed two new teams prior to the 2005-06 season: the Florida Seals and the Pee Dee Cyclones. After two subpar seasons, winning just 32 out of 112 games, the struggling franchise could not reach an agreement on a new lease. With no viable options in South Carolina, owner Bob Kerzner opted to move the franchise to Winston-Salem ahead of the 2007-08 season.

Their first season in North Carolina did not produce spectacular results. While they finished next to last in the league, they still earned a postseason appearance. It was, however, a brief appearance as the Jacksonville Barracudas eliminated the Cyclones in two straight games. Adding insult was the fact that their attendance was below where it had been before the relocation. The situation wasn't dire, but the team needed a change in fortune.

While their offense improved in 2008-09, their position in the standings did not. A last-place finish meant no playoffs. Attendance was stable when compared to the season before, but far from what the team needed in order to be financially stable. Following the end of their second season in Winston-Salem, the Cyclones folded.

CAROLINA THUNDERBIRDS (FPHL; 2017-PRESENT)

As the summer of 2016 crept towards its twilight, the Federal Hockey League (now known as the Federal Prospects Hockey

League) announced that it would place a new expansion team in Winston-Salem. Set to begin play in the 2017-18 season, the team brought back the Thunderbirds namesake and hired Andre Niec to run the bench. The team played well in their first season, posting a 30-24-0-2 record to earn a third-place finish. Josh Pietrantonio led the team with 56 points; Michael Bunn—a Wake Forest native—was the top goal scorer with 27. The Thunderbirds used six goaltenders through the course of the season, four of which posted winning records.

Not a bad start.

The campaign came to a premature end when they suffered a sweep in the opening round of the playoffs, but the team had established roots in the city. During their first season, the Thunderbirds drew an average of just over 2,200 fans per game—the best mark in the league—including a sellout for their first home game of the year. The season also saw the first in what would become a bit of a tradition. During a game in late January 2018, Niec became incensed at the officials over a disputed call. He subsequently swung a stick at one official and the league responded by suspending the coach.

More on that tradition later.

The team's performance grew by leaps and bounds in 2018-19. Pietrantonio picked up 83 points to lead the team; his 27 goals tied with Bunn for best on the roster. Slovakian netminder Christian Pavlas stabilized the goaltending, appearing in 46 games, going 30-3-2 with a goals against average of 1.77 and a .932 save percentage as well as 5 shutouts, all of which led the league. The Thunderbirds finished at the top of the standings and brought home a handful of individual awards, including:

- Christian Pavlac - Goaltender of the Year
- Mike Baker - Defenseman of the Year
- Andre Niec - Coach of the Year
- Josh Pietrantonio - League MVP

Now, let's get back to that tradition. During a game against Port Huron Prowlers—a game that the Thunderbirds won 6-0—Niec was ejected and subsequently suspended for six games after an altercation with the officials. Making the best of the situation, the team elected to make head trainer Karolina Huvarova interim head coach. With this, Huvarova became the first European woman to coach a men's professional hockey team. A review of the actions leading to Niec's suspension led the league to reduce it from six games to four.

As for Huvarova's tenure, the Thunderbirds went 3-0-0-1. That's impressive, even over such a short period of time.

With such an eventful season behind them, the true test for the Thunderbirds came in the playoffs. The opening round pitted them against Port Huron, and Carolina took the series in two games. The contests were tight, with both Carolina victories being one-goal affairs. Also important to note is that coach Niec did not get suspended. The finals matched the Thunderbirds against the Elmira Enforcers, the second-best team during the regular season.

I shouldn't neglect to say that they still finished 50 points behind Carolina.

Game one proved to be a harbinger as the Thunderbirds downed the Enforcers by a score of 7-3. Game two was tighter, but Carolina once again prevailed, this time by a final of 4-3. Elmira got their revenger in the third game, putting up seven goals of their own and, while the fourth game was close, Carolina won 4-3 and captured the Commissioner's Cup as league champions. Thanks to their success, the team saw a bump in attendance, averaging 2,700 fans per game.

The 2019-20 season brought challenges to the team, namely the loss of both Pietrantonio and Pavlac. With their absence, a trio of Czech-born players took over. Petr Panacek was Carolina's top scorer, picking up 69 points in 46 games; Jan Salak led the team with 29 goals while defenseman Daniel Klinecky racked up 18 goals and 60 points. The goaltending situation wasn't as clear cut as the team dressed eight netminders during the season, with none appearing in more than 23 games.

There were, however, three that stood out:

- Patrik Polivka: 11-2-0; 2.23 GAA; .912 SV%; 0 SO
- Henry Dill: 9-1-1; 1.72 GAA; .938 SV%; 3 SO
- Jacob Mullen: 9-2-2; 2.51 GAA; .910 SV%; 2 SO

As for Niec, he kept the tradition alive. During the third period of a game against the Columbus River Dragons, with the Thunderbirds ahead 7-2, tensions boiled over. Both Niec and Columbus coach Jerome Bechard walked onto the ice, hellbent on fisticuffs. River Dragons defenseman Nick Wright challenged Niec, resulting in a full-on brawl breaking out. The coaches never came to blows, though Niec wound up on Columbus' bench where an opposing player set upon him. Niec retaliated, losing his shirt in the process.

By the time officials restored order, they assessed 133 penalty minutes along with multiple suspensions. Niec, naturally, received an eight-game ban.

The Thunderbirds season, however, would not be derailed by such displays. The team sat atop the league with a record of 35-6-0-5 when the COVID-19 pandemic led to the remainder of the season being cancelled.

The pandemic also disrupted the 2020-21 FPHL season, delaying its start until February 2021. When the dust settled, just four of the league's teams—including the Thunderbirds—opted to take part in the shortened season. Another issue arose for Carolina, namely the lack of availability of their home arena. With the ice at the Winston-Salem Fairgrounds Annex removed to accommodate previously scheduled events, the Thunderbirds would play all of their games on the road. This also forced the team to conduct their practices in Greensboro, nearly 30 miles away.

Carolina competed in 20 games, the fewest of the four active teams. Despite this, they accumulated three more points than Port Huron, who took part in 24 contests. Their 10-9-0-1 record wasn't particularly impressive, though—given the circumstances—it wasn't as disastrous a campaign as it could have been. Forwards Josh Koepplinger and Petr Panacek led the team with 25 points, while Tom Tsicos and Fred Hein both scored a team-best 13 goals. Of the three goaltenders used during the season, Chris Paulin gave the best results with a record of 5-1.

Following the season, the team announced Niec would depart from the Thunderbirds after a successful stint as their coach. The NHL's Florida Panthers hired Niec to serve as a European scout, allowing him to stay in hockey and work from his home in the Czech Republic. Carolina took their time in searching for their next coach, knowing the impact that Niec had. Ultimately, they hired Garrett Rutledge, who served as the video coach of the OHL's Saginaw Spirit for two seasons.

CHAPTER FOUR

Blue Ridge Breakaway

NORTH CAROLINA'S Blue Ridge Mountains are a popular tourist area, renowned for the area's natural beauty. From the famed Blue Ridge Parkway to the Biltmore Estate; Grandfather Mountain to the Linville Falls, there are countless things the area is known for. What many don't know is that the area has a history of professional ice hockey that goes back nearly four decades. We'll start with a team that set up shop in possibly the most unlikely of markets.

PINEBRIDGE BUCKS (ACHL; 1983-85)

This entry, to me, is by far the most interesting. That's not to diminish any of the others but to emphasize just how unexpected, strange, and—ultimately—amazing this story is. I don't want to oversell it, so I'll just get right into it.

Thirteen miles south of the North Carolina-Tennessee border sits the town of Spruce Pine. The town—nestled in the Blue Ridge Mountains—was originally founded as a railroad hub back in 1907. Picturesque and small (the town covers just under five square miles), Spruce Pine's population in the early 1980s hovered around 2,000. It's a beautiful town that's a great place to visit; is it not, however, the type of place you would ever expect to find a professional hockey team.

Yet here we are.

Robert Bailey, a local and the founder of Buck Stoves, wanted to give something to the community. More than that, he wanted to give the people of Spruce Pine something to do. When he heard that an old school property was available for purchase, Bailey and his business partner, Alvin Barier, jumped at the opportunity. The property would become a multi-purpose facility, housing a restaurant, an inn, and the largest indoor ice rink in the state. The complex—which began construction in 1983—became known as the Pinebridge Coliseum, taking its namesake from the bridge that connected downtown to the building.[1]

Despite the presence of the rink, there was never a plan for the complex to serve as the home to a hockey team. Bailey did, however, have the idea of using the ice to host a hockey school; he reached out to Carolina Thunderbirds owner/GM/coach Rick Dudley, hoping he would run the endeavor. While Dudley had too much on his plate to accept, he visited Spruce Pine and, by the time he left, decided that the Pinebridge Coliseum would make a suitable home for an ACHL team. With a $5,000 check cut to the league, the Pinebridge Bucks were born. Dudley brought in former NHL center Don Luce as head coach and the process of recruiting players for the 1983-84 season began.

Bailey and Barrier knew the team wouldn't be a cash cow, but that was okay. There was hope that the team would draw both attention and visitors to Spruce Pine, the smallest town to host a pro hockey team. With the bottom line in mind, the Bucks operated on a tight budget. The arena staff was made up entirely of volunteers, saving the excess cash required to hire a full staff. For his part, Barrier served as a jack of all trades, doing everything from driving the Zamboni to completing miscellaneous repairs at the facility.[2]

Montreal native Rob Clavette was a standout in the inaugural season, notching 53 goals and 131 points in 72 games. Fellow winger Dave MacQueen was the team's top goal scorer, picking up 54 and adding an equal number of assists. Outside of Clavette and MacQueen, the Bucks had four other players score at least 30 goals, with two of them eclipsing the 40-goal mark. Despite the potent offense, Pinebridge finished second-to-last in the league. They may well have finished at the bottom if not for the Birmingham Bulls folding just three games into the season.

Defense and goaltending proved to be areas of opportunity for the Bucks. Surrendering a league-high 422 goals during the season, they would have little chance of success moving forward if they didn't solidify this weakness. As it turned out, there almost wasn't another season for the Bucks. Bailey had become disenfranchised with the state of the league; more directly, he didn't agree with the tactics of a handful of other owners. A marathon conversation with Dudley eventually persuaded Bailey to keep the Bucks around for a second season.

"I spent from 10 AM to 4 AM one night convincing him to spend another year in the league because if he backed out, Utica would want out because they didn't want to be in a four-team league and we couldn't have a three-team league. I convinced him to spend another year in the league, and he did it more for me than anything else."

-Rick Dudley[3]

With the team committed to the 1984-85 ACHL season, training got underway. Future Carolina Thunderbirds and Team USA goalie Ray LeBlanc joined the team, making his professional debut. Once again, Clavette led the team with 114 points. Newcomer Scott Robins was the top goal scorer, netting 53. Second year Buck Frank Perkins chipped in 15 goals and 70 points from the blueline while also racking up an impressive 233 penalty minutes.

LeBlanc handled most of the goaltending workload, appearing in 40 games and posting a record of 18-21-0. Steve Heittola filled in admirably as the backup, going 13-8-0 in 28 appearances and posting one shutout (the first and only in Bucks team history). The Bucks played a better all-around defensive game, cutting their goals against by an astounding 124. The effort earned them a berth in the playoffs and their fans the opportunity to witness postseason hockey. It was a huge step forward for the small market team.

The opening round gave the Bucks a matchup against the defending champion Erie Golden Blades. After dropping the first game 6-2, Pinebridge responding with a 5-3 victory. The teams went back and forth through the next two games, leaving the series tied at 2-2 heading into the fifth game. Erie prevailed, winning the next two games by a combined score of 10-6, ending the Bucks' run. Clavette once again led the way, picking up 6 goals and 10 points in 6 playoff contests.

Following the season, Bailey made the decision to pull the plug on the team. While the team had a short lifespan, they managed to leave a lasting legacy. This primarily stems from the fact that they helped keep the ACHL from collapsing, which, in turn, led to the creation of the ECHL, a league that is still active today. They also introduced the game to a new and unlikely market and, for a brief time, gave the people of Spruce Pine something to rally behind.

"Who would have ever thought that Spruce Pine would have its own hockey team? But we did, and people came from all over to see it."

-Spruce Pine resident George Parker[4]

I'll close this section with what is possibly my favorite story relating to the Bucks. Sometime in 1984, the Carolina Thunderbirds came to town for a game. Their bus driver, unwilling to navigate the twisting mountain road, pulled onto the shoulder. Someone from the Thunderbirds—Dudley, perhaps—called the Bucks, who sent someone down to drive the bus up for them. The game went on as scheduled, though there's no record of who drove the bus back down.

ASHEVILLE SMOKE (UHL; 1998-2002)

The Brantford Smoke—a founding member of the United Hockey League—had a decent run in southwestern Ontario. Over seven seasons, the Smoke reached the playoffs in all but one. During that span they finished atop the league standings once and captured the Colonial Cup as league champions in 1993. Despite these successes, the team regularly finished with attendance near the bottom of the league. Their last season in Canada was one of their worst, as they averaged 1,424 fans per game; the Quad City Mallards—the league's top draw—averaged 7,650.

Team owners Andy and Dan Wilhelm began looking for a new home for the Smoke. Citing the ability to break into a new market and a lack of pro sports competition, the brothers opted to move their team to Asheville. Taking up residence in the Asheville Civic Center, the Wilhelms installed ice making equipment and set about assembling their team. Since none of the previous year's Brantford squad made the move to Asheville, they had to start from scratch. The first step was finding a coach, and they found one with the biggest surname in hockey: Gretzky.

The team hired Keith Gretzky—one of The Great One's younger brothers—as their head coach. With training camp looming, Gretzky found his roster in need of help down the middle. That help, as luck would have it, came from the youngest Gretzky brother, Brent. During a phone conversation where Brent expressed his displeasure with playing in Europe,

Keith took a chance and offered his brother a contract[5]. Brent, who put up 62 points in 37 games while playing in Austria during the 1997-98 season, also appeared in 13 games with the Tampa Bay Lightning between 1993-1995.

With the puck dropping on the 1998-99 season, the Smoke suffered through ups and downs. This new incarnation finished with a worse record than the last season in Brantford, but still qualified for the postseason. Twenty-seven-year-old Lindsay Vallis paced the team with 100 points; center Shawn Ulrich led the Smoke with 39 goals. Brent Gretzky—between stints in the AHL and IHL—suited up in 32 games for Asheville and posted 28 goals and 70 points. This placed him third in team scoring despite appearing in fewer than half of the Smoke's games.

There was no shortage of sandpaper on the roster with three players hitting triple digits in penalty minutes. Left wing Kris Schultz led the way with 281; the aptly named Wade Welte was next up with 258 and defenseman Rob Milliken came in third with 119. Sorel, Quebec native Danny Laviolette was the team's top netminder, posting a 23-17-2 record in 44 games played. The Smoke finished at 36-35-0-3, good enough for second place in the Eastern Division. They earned a playoff matchup against the defending champion Quad City Mallards, a series that ended with Asheville being swept.

While they came up short in the postseason, the year was a success for the newcomers. They posted the third-best attendance in the league, with an average of 3,362 fans per game, more than twice what the franchise drew during its last season in Ontario. Their new fans had accepted the Smoke, and the team looked to build on that as they headed into the 1999-2000 season. Roster turnover cost the team Laviolette and left the bulk of goaltending duty to Dan McIntyre. The leading scorers, however, remained largely unchanged.

The Smoke's second season in Asheville got off to a very inauspicious start when their home opener had to be postponed. An issue with the refrigeration equipment in the Civic Center led to the ice not being—well, ice. They were able to fix the situation, but that wasn't the end of the building's issues. A November 10 contest had to be rescheduled following a power failure. Fans were rightfully unsure about heading out for games, not knowing if some type of arena problem would end the evening's festivities before they could start.

When they were able to play, the team's performance was on par compared to the previous year. They finished slightly lower in the standings but still earned the right to compete in the postseason. This was thanks to a strong performance from Gretzky (36 goals, 128 points) and offensive depth that provided seven 20-goal scorers. Unfortunately, the result was the same as the prior season: a first round sweep. They hadn't regressed, but they weren't seeing the progress they hoped for.

Attendance suffered—not helped by the early season facility issues—though the team still averaged a respectable 3,036 fans per game. With the 26-year-old Civic Center showing its age, Dan Wilhelm proposed the construction of a new arena in Asheville[6]. While funding for such an endeavor was hard to come by, Wilhelm also planned to upgrade the team's current home. The hope was to eliminate the functionality issues that were multiplying and to provide a better experience for the fans. Despite losing over $100,000[7] because of postponements, Wilhelm remained committed to keeping the team in Buncombe County.

In July 2000, Pat Bingham replaced Keith Gretzky as the Smoke's coach. One of Bingham's focus areas was bringing in larger players to win puck battles, screen goalies, and play a gritty, hard-nosed game. They would also have to overcome the loss of Brent Gretzky and his offensive output. Once the 2000-01 season was underway, it became clear that the change in mindset had worked for the better. The team shot to the top of the newly formed Southeast Division, amassing 45 wins and finishing second overall in the league.

New arrival Dominic Maltais led the Smoke with 40 goals and 101 points. They finished with 297 goals, good for second overall, while improving to become the sixth-best defensive team. Bingham's desire for more physicality also came to fruition. The Smoke became the most penalized team in the league (2507 penalty minutes), led by a prodigious 401 from winger Bruce Watson. The team received reliable goaltending from Brent Belecki, owner of a 34-17-4 record and one shutout.

Their regular season performance gave Asheville a much more favorable spot in the playoffs. They made the most out of it, eliminating the Knoxville Speed in three straight, outscoring their opponent 14-4. While the second round brought a new opponent—the New Haven Knights—the results were much the same. Asheville won in a sweep while outscoring the New Haven 12-6. For the first time since relocating, the Smoke had fought their way to the Colonial Cup Finals.

The championship series proved to be a challenge, pitting the Smoke against Quad City, the league's best regular season team. Their dominance carried into the finals and the Mallards bested Asheville in five games. Winger J. C. Ruid was the Smoke's best postseason offensive threat, notching 11 goals and 16 points over 11 games. While their on-ice performance improved—and the take from seven home playoff games was nice for ownership—attendance fell for the second consecutive year. Asheville finished with an average of 2,604 fan per game, down 432 from the year before.

Change was in store for the Smoke prior to the 2001-02 season as the recently retired Shawn Ulrich—who had been with the team since their move—replaced Bingham behind the bench. He promptly made additions to his roster, bringing in wingers Jeff Petruic and Jean-Francois Dufour along with goaltender Blaine Russell, a 6th round pick of the Mighty Ducks of Anaheim in 1996. The Smoke also welcomed a co-tenant at the Civic Center when Asheville landed a team in the National Basketball Development League (NBDL).

The campaign started off well enough as Asheville opened with two wins over the Knoxville Speed. Things quickly took a downward turn when the Smoke went on a four-game losing streak before settling into a trend of following a short winning streak with a short losing streak. The backbreaker came at the beginning of March when Asheville went nine games without a win, effectively tanking their season. Petruic and Dufour acquitted themselves well, posting 114 and 105 points, respectively. Russell led the team's goaltenders with 21 wins and two shutouts.

Attendance dropped again, settling at an average of 2,382 for the season. In mid-2002, Wilhelm filed for bankruptcy, a hardship that cast doubt on the Smoke's future. It's important to note that travel costs didn't help the team either, since the closest UHL franchise was the Knoxville Speed, located 116 miles west. The Winston-Salem IceHawks were just 145 miles away but, after they relocated in 1999, that left the average travel distance at 672 miles one-way. That's not a lot when you consider chartered planes but, when you're dealing strictly with buses, it becomes much more costly.

Though the team made a bid to join the ACHL—a move that would have significantly reduced travel expenses—it failed to materialize and the Smoke ceased operations.

ASHEVILLE ACES (SPHL; 2004-05)

In the spring of 2004, almost two years after the Smoke faded into obscurity, the Southern Professional Hockey League set up shop in Asheville. Jeff Brubaker—who had coached the Greensboro Monarchs for six years and the Greensboro Generals for one—came in as head coach and general manager. The team agreed to terms on a three-year lease with the Asheville Civic Center, which actually played a role in the SPHL coming to town. The South East Hockey League sought to establish a team in Asheville during this time, but city officials mandated that any team taking residence in the Civic Center be in a league of at least six teams, to help ensure financial viability. With only four teams, the SEHL had to bow out, so the SPHL came to town.

Dubbed the Aces, Asheville's new team showed promise early, opening the season with a 3-0 victory over Fayetteville. They went on to win six of their first ten games, only to falter down the stretch and lose 14 of their last 20. The team finished second-to-last, thanks only to an abysmal campaign from Winston-Salem. Compounding the Aces' woes was poor attendance. When you couple that with the aging Civic Center and a poor lease, the outlook for the team was just as ugly is their finish in the standings.

Truth be told, nothing was as ugly as the Aces' lease agreement. Based on a per-game sliding scale, the team's rent was lower the higher the attendance. Conversely, games with fewer fans meant a higher payment. On average, the Aces drew just over 1,200 per game. That figure, however, includes close to 500 complimentary tickets, leaving the paid attendance at 767 per game. As a result, the team's 28 home games netted the city over $200,000.[8]

For that tidy sum, the Aces paid for the rights to play in the 30-year-old Civic Center, a venue badly in need of upgrades. The team's owners—claiming losses in excess of $100,000—sought to restructure the lease in order to gain a more even balance. City leaders, citing the team's unpaid debt of $18,000, were hesitant to re-open negotiations. With the situation at a stalemate, the Aces announced they were immediately suspending operations and would not take part in the 2005-06 SPHL season. They would never resume play.

CHAPTER FIVE

Capital Incursion

RALEIGH ICECAPS (ECHL; 1991-98)

THIS ONE IS special to me.

While I had been watching hockey on television for years, the IceCaps represented my first opportunity to see the game live. My grandmother was going to take me to my first game but, when she didn't feel up to it, my grandfather stepped in. While he had a passing knowledge of hockey, he was a baseball guy, and I did not know how he would respond to it. As it turned out, he loved it.

I can still remember walking up to the ticket booth, plunking down $5, and passing hills of shaved ice as we made our way inside. My excitement began boiling when we hit the dimly lit concourse. The smells of burgers, pizza, and barbecue sandwiches mingled in the cool air. I sat, mesmerized, during warm-ups, my young mind unable to comprehend the fact that I was about to witness a hockey game live and in person. Oddly enough, the one thing I can't remember is the final score, or if the IceCaps even won. It didn't matter; they could have lost 20-0 and I still would have had the time of my life.

In the subsequent years, IceCaps games became a staple. I remember one game specifically—a matchup against the South Carolina Stingrays—where an overzealous kid stepped dead-center in my friend Dennis' hot dog. He had placed it down for just a moment to get situated and, in an instant, the poor frankfurter met a grisly under a wayward Converse. Adding insult to injury, the IceCaps lost the game.

Rest in peace, hot dog. Sadly, your death was in vain.

I got my driver's license during the 1997-98 season, meaning that I could go to games whenever I wanted, bearing schoolwork and having enough cash for gas and a ticket. This also led to my least-fond memory of attending games. I walked out to the parking lot after a game and found a man talking to an arena worker; someone had broken into his car. As I continued walking, I saw more people whose vehicles had been vandalized. "Wow," I thought, "thank God it wasn't me."

Then, I got to my car.

Sure enough, I found the driver's window smashed and small chunks of safety glass were all over the place. Inside, the thief had taken the CD player, along with my copy of Re-Load. All that was bad, but the worst part? Vacuuming up all those pieces of glass. I was still finding pieces years later.

My first experience playing any sort of organized hockey was in the Raleigh Parks & Recreation league. The first event was an open practice led by none other than IceCaps forward Jimmy Powers. The day was fully of shooting drills and what felt like ten hours of breakaways; as the only goalie present, it was exhausting, but I managed to stop a handful of shots fired by a pro, so there's that.

Now that some of that backstory is out of the way, let's get to the team.

The duo of Miles Wolff and Pete Bock—experienced with minor-league baseball teams—secured an expansion franchise in Raleigh with the East Coast Hockey League in 1991. Dubbed the Raleigh IceCaps, the team signed a lease to play their home games at Dorton Arena, located on the North Carolina State Fairgrounds.

This is where that minor-league hockey magic comes into play.

First opened in 1952, Dorton Arena was originally designed to host livestock events so, naturally, was not equipped with the hardware to make or maintain ice. Unwilling to dig up the arena's floor and install the required equipment, the owners opted to use a system of mats to create the ice.[1] While suitable for some applications, professional hockey was not one of them, and the ice at Dorton Arena quickly developed a reputation as the worst in the league.

Not to be outdone by subpar ice, the IceCaps got off to an awful start, dropping their first four games and being outscored 34-12 in the process. After defeating the Knoxville Cherokees in their fifth game, the team started to find their rhythm. They traded wins and losses but never completely derailed. Head coach Kurt Kleinendorst steered them through the worst of it and they finished their first year in fifth place in the East Division with a 25-33-3-3 record. They hosted the Hampton Roads Admirals in the first round of the playoffs, winning the opener before losing three straight.

Despite the fact that this marked the first foray of professional hockey into the state's capital, the IceCaps fared well at the box office. An average of 4,773 fans attended home games, good enough for the sixth-best attendance number in the 15-team league. Standout players from the inaugural season included center Rick Barkovich with 67 points and winger

Jimmy Powers—who, you'll remember, I made numerous saves on in rec league practice—with a team-best 34 goals. The IceCaps didn't shy away from the rough stuff either, as three players (Barry Nieckar, Sylvain Mayer, and Barkovich) hit triple digits in penalty minutes.

I would like to take a moment to mention that Mayer racked up 104 penalty minutes. That doesn't sound impressive until you consider that he only appeared in six games for Raleigh after arriving in a trade with Louisville. For what it's worth, he only picked up six penalty minutes in two games before the trade.

Maybe it was the bad ice.

The IceCaps got off to a much better start in the 1992-92 season, opening with a 6-game winning streak. Overall, their play was consistently at a higher level than the year before. A large factor in this was the emergence of left wing Lyle Wild-goose. Acquired in a 1991 trade with Richmond, the Sudbury, Ontario native led the IceCaps in goals (36) and points (86). Powers continued his strong play, picking up 28 goals and 77 points while Alan Leggett provided strong, two-way play from the blueline with 16 goals and 46 points.

The goaltending picture was also far less cluttered during the second season. While Raleigh dressed six netminders during their inaugural year, they now had a reliable tandem in Stan Reddick and Jim Mill. Their improved performance elevated the IceCaps to a third place division finish and a second consecutive postseason appearance. Following a first round bye, they defeated Hampton Roads before being eliminated by the Wheeling Thunderbirds. No championship, but it was a big step forward for the team, including raising their average attendance to 5,062.

The 1993-94 season found the IceCaps off to another hot start, winning eight of their first ten games. They finished the year with a five-game winning streak, which included a 10-3 win over Huntington. Wildgoose once again led the way, his 40 goals and 86 points both tops on the team. Future NHL tough guy Krzysztof Oliwa made his North American debut, splitting time between Raleigh and Albany of the AHL. There was a shuffle in goal as former NHL netminders Matt DelGuidice and Chad Erickson combined for 63 appearances and 37 wins.

They finished the year second in the East Division, a single point behind Hampton Roads. Attendance was still strong, though it dipped slightly, giving the IceCaps a season average of 4,954 fans. Their solid play continued into the playoffs, carrying them past the Roanoke Express, Greensboro Monarchs, and Birmingham Bulls, and earning them a berth in the Riley Cup Finals. They clashed with the defending champion Toledo Storm, but could not unseat them. The IceCaps had made strides in their third season and seemed poised to challenge the league's best again.

The 1994-95 season, however, would prove challenging. Kleinendorst resigned in May 1994 to take an assistant coaching position with the IHL's San Diego Gulls; his replacement was the recently retired Barkovich. Things got off to a rocky start for the new coach and improved little as the season wore on. The IceCaps struggled offensively, finishing with a second-worst 239 goals scored over the 68-game campaign. While averaging 3.5 goals per game doesn't sound bad, the team surrendered 4.3 goals against, on average.

By season's end, Raleigh sat dead last in their division, second to last in the league, and missed the playoffs for the first time. The silver lining—if there was one—came in a small attendance bump, as the team finished with over 5,000 fans per game. Ownership let Barkovich go and replaced him with the man who he replaced one year earlier, when Kleinendorst signed a three-year contract with the team. Wildgoose, who had announced his retirement after Barkovich left, decided to return when Kleinendorst returned. There would be much work to do as Wildgoose was one of a handful of returning players.

Sadly, the return of the coach who had led them to the finals in 1994 didn't yield huge returns. The IceCaps opened the 1995-96 season with a six-game road trip and lost every one. Things didn't improve upon their return to Dorton Arena as they lost their first four home games. Despite a 72 point performance from Wildgoose, Raleigh struggled mightily on offense, finishing with a league-worst 215 goals scored. They managed to reduce their goals against by 29, but their anemic offense was woefully inadequate compared to their competition.

The IceCaps won four of their last five games, just enough to squeak into the playoffs. Facing off against the Tallahassee Tiger Sharks, Raleigh won the first game of the series before dropping three straight and being eliminated. A return to the postseason was certainly nice, but it was hardly the result the team hoped for. The fans evidently felt the same way, witnessed by attendance dropping to 4,004 per game, their lowest total ever. Hope for an improved performance moving forward took a hit when Wildgoose retired for good, finishing his IceCaps career with 150 goals and 360 points in 306 games.

Raleigh improved in the 1996-97 season, finishing with seven more wins than the year before. Unfortunately, with the league expanding to 23 teams, their performance wasn't enough to earn them a berth in the playoffs. Attendance took a noticeable dip, falling to 3,091, setting a new franchise low. There was a bright spot for the team as second-year IceCap Darren Colbourne posted a 53 goal, 101 point effort, both team records. The team also saw a brief appearance by goal-tender Steve Passmore, who would go on to appear in 93 NHL games with the Edmonton Oilers, Chicago Blackhawks, and Los Angeles Kings.

This season also marked the lone professional season for winger Jason Karmanos, whose father would soon make an announcement that would change the North Carolina hockey landscape. On May 6, 1997, Peter Karmanos—Jason's father and owner of the NHL's Hartford Whalers—declared that he was moving his team to Raleigh. We'll dive deeper into that soon; for now, we'll focus on the effect that the announcement had on the IceCaps. The imminent arrival of an NHL franchise in Raleigh called the long-term viability of the ECHL team into question; whatever the future held, there would be a new shot caller for the team. Kleinendorst departed after accepting a job in England; in his stead came first-time head coach Dan Wiebe.

Initially, the plans were for the IceCaps to remain in Raleigh[2] for at least two years. That, however, did not come to pass. The team issued an official announcement in September that, upon completion of the 1997-98 season, the IceCaps would relocate to Augusta, Georgia. With that pall over their heads, the team took to the ice and promptly lost their first four games and seven of their first ten. Attendance plummeted, falling to under 2,000 per game and placing Raleigh dead last in the league. They finished the year with the fourth-worst record and missed the playoffs for the second season in a row.

After relocation, the team—now known as the Lynx—spent a decade in Augusta before folding in the middle of the 2008-09 season.

THE NHL EXPANSION BID

The 1990s brought a new era of growth for the NHL. The first half of the decade witnessed the league adding five new markets—San Jose, Ottawa, Tampa Bay, Miami, and Anaheim —and looking to increase their footprint before the decade drew to a close. With cities such as Nashville, Tennessee, Houston, Texas, and Columbus, Ohio vying for expansion franchises, mayor Tom Fetzer decided to throw Raleigh into the mix. It made sense; the city was booming and there was no major-league competition in town. They just needed two things: an arena and a potential owner.

The arena part was taken care of; well, sort of. Going back to the mid-1980s, North Carolina State University had been kicking the idea around of building a new arena for the Wolf-pack basketball team. In 1995, the North Carolina General Assembly created the Centennial Authority, a body tasked with managing all aspects of the proposed facility. They promptly decided that, to get the best return on investment, the arena should be multi-purpose. Talk began of bringing a hockey team on board as a tenant and, with the NHL seeking to expand, the city threw its hat in the ring. Still, they needed an owner.

Initial speculation pointed to Charlotte Hornets' owner, George Shinn. This, however, never materialized and Shinn went a different route, submitting an expansion application for Hampton Roads, Virginia, in the fall of 1996. Still, this didn't spell doom for Raleigh's bid since the NHL was consid-ering adding up to four new teams. On the other hand, it left them without an owner for the perspective team. That changed in October 1996, when Felix Sabates, Jr., a Charlotte businessman, came on board. With urging from city leaders, Sabates assembled an ownership group and provided the NHL mandated $100,000 application fee.

Things, however, quickly began to sour.

Sabates, a hot-tempered racing team owner who never hesitated to bump heads with NASCAR officials, soon felt that the city wasn't sincerely committed to bringing an NHL team to Raleigh. The main point of contention stemmed from questions about funding the new arena. Wake County and the City of Raleigh had committed $28 millions towards the arena project, a figure that Mayor Fetzer hesitated to increase in order to match the rising projection of the facility's cost. Supporters of the bid proposed using a hotel tax to raise funds, a motion that Fetzer shot down during a city council meeting.

"I felt this guy had put a dagger in my heart. He also put a dagger in the heart of the community."
Felix Sabates, Jr.[3]

The situation continued to worsen despite the fact that Fetzer and Sabates had not held a face-to-face meeting to discuss these issues. The businessman was so eager to speak with the mayor that he attempted—fruitlessly—to speak with him at a Carolina Panthers game both men were attending. Both parties felt that they had made adequate concessions, and neither was willing to yield more ground. The city was concerned about getting into a financial boondoggle, while the expansion group doubted that city and county officials were vigilant concerning the future of the bid that they initiated. While publicly stating that he was leaning towards pulling out, Sabates elected to wait until after a December 6 meeting with NHL Commissioner Gary Bettman.

During this time, the city council pressured the Centennial Authority to downsize the proposed arena in an effort to cut costs. The council felt the arena would be financially viable on a smaller scale and with no NHL team as a tenant. The Authority countered that, with no pro team, the facility would need to host a large amount of concerts and other events to make the building profitable for all involved. Ideas bounced around, ranging from an AHL expansion team to inviting the Raleigh IceCaps to act as a tenant[4] in the new arena.

With all the foot dragging, a scheduled vote on the arena was pushed back from mid-January to early February 1997. That gave Sabates' group less than two weeks before the NHL executive committee was set to meet again to discuss expansion. Still, the group was hopeful and felt they had at least a good a shot as any of the others vying for a team. With the league set to make a final decision on new markets during the first week of March, the clock was ticking fast. If an agreement on arena funding couldn't be reached, the expansion bid would be dead in the water.

With lease and funding qualms burning like a brushfire, Sabates went to New York to make his pitch to Bettman and the executive committee. Bettman also extended invitations to current owners who were interested in sitting in. Peter Karmanos—owner of the struggling Hartford Whalers—was there. Sabates laid out, in extensive detail, why Raleigh was ripe for an NHL team. He made assurances—he was, after all, a businessman—and did everything he could to sell the league on the city and its surrounding communities.

Then, just a few weeks later, Sabates pulled his bid, ending the months-long expansion drama. His presentation had not been in vain, however. Regardless of how the league perceived his pitch, one man was impressed with what he had heard: Karmanos.

CHAPTER SIX

Flinging Fists in Fayetteville

FAYETTEVILLE FORCE (CHL; 1997-2001)

THE MID-1990S REPRESENTED a period of growth for the Central Hockey League. Prior to the start of the 1996-97 season, the league grew from six teams to ten and was seeking to expand their reach further east. Bill Coffey, who helped start the ECHL, applied for a franchise to be located in Fayetteville. Seeing a large, untapped region—including Fort Bragg—the league awarded a team to Coffey, who dubbed the new franchise the Fayetteville Force. They would begin play in the 1997-98 CHL season with the newly opened Crown Coliseum serving as their home rink.

Coffey hired Alan May, a retired player who spent parts of eight seasons in the NHL, to coach the new team. They assembled their roster, and the Force opened their inaugural season with a 6-5 victory over the Huntsville Channel Cats. The luster quickly faded as they lost their next game—while surrendering 11 goals—and emerged from their first ten games with a record of 4-6. The team was unable to maintain their footing during the season and fell into a ten-game losing streak. They recovered briefly, stringing together a five-game winning streak, though this run preceded a string of 13 straight losses.

Despite finishing at the bottom of their division, the Force averaged 3,987 fans for each home game, placing them in the middle of the league. Jeffrey Azar emerged as the team's offensive leader, posting 39 goals and 75 points in 68 games. The winger's performance placed him in a tie for seventh place in league goal scoring, the only Fayetteville player to crack the top ten of any major category. Aaron Boh also had an impressive campaign; the defenseman put up 15 goals and 58 points in just 56 games. As is common in minor-league hockey, significant roster turnover would reshape the team prior to the 1998-99 season.

May departed as coach, replaced by David Lohrei. Azar and Boh were also gone; Azar signing with the Winston-Salem IceHawks while Boh went to the IHL's Fort Wayne Komets. The most important change proved to be the arrival of Minnesota-born left wing Chad Remackel. Appearing in all 70 games during his lone season with the Force, Remackel posted 36 goals and 103 points, the latter a team record which was never broken. Fayetteville racked up ten more wins than they had in their first season and gained 25 points in the standings, but still failed to qualify for postseason play.

Remackel's departure prior to the 1999-2000 season opened the door for a new leader; one emerged, though it wasn't a forward. Defenseman Brett Colborne tallied 21 goals and 81 points while also providing solid defensive play. Justin Tomberlin, a former member of the Raleigh IceCaps, became the team's sniper, netting 43 goals. Nathan Grobins—coming off of two phenomenal seasons with the Fort Worth Fire— came in, hoping to stabilize the goaltending. It worked; Grobins posted a 24-11-1 record with the Force, stopping 91% of the shots he faced while posting two shutouts.

Finishing with a 45-22-3 record, this would be the team's

most successful season. Claiming the top spot in not only their division but the entire league, the Force reached the playoffs for the first time and did so as favorites to win it all. They opened the postseason against the Macon Whoopee (not to be confused with the old Macon Whoopees of the SHL; God bless the minor leagues), a team that finished 15 points lower in the standings. In an example of the worst possible timing, the offensive and defensive acumen that carried Fayetteville through the regular season completely evaporated. Macon, who lost to the Force in their last game of the regular season, won the series 3-1; Fayetteville managed just five goals in the four game set.

Even with this premature end, the 1999-00 season provided several highlights for the team. On January 25, 2000, Fayetteville hosted the inter-league CHL/WCHL All-Star Game, an event that drew 6,128 spectators to the Coliseum. This was despite the fact that a massive snowstorm had struck North Carolina, leaving many parts of Fayetteville under 10-12 inches of snow. The team also captured a pair of individual awards as Colborne was named 'Defenseman of the Year' while Lohrei brought home the Commissioner's Trophy as coach of the year. Overall attendance, however, was down, and the Force finished ninth out of 11 teams.

Following the season, Lohrei departed for coaching job in the ECHL, the same league that new head coach Todd Gordon hailed from. Colborne, Tomberlin, and Grobins also left during the summer. Seeking to replace some of the lost offense, the Force brought in veteran center Darryl Noren, the same Darryl Noren that previously played for the Greensboro Monarchs and Charlotte Checkers. As the 2000-01 season got underway, the team noticeably regressed. Trading wins and losses, blending unbeaten streaks into winless streaks, Fayetteville struggled to stay relevant.

They kept their heads above water long enough to secure a spot in the 2001 playoffs, though the Columbus Cottonmouths eliminated them in a five-game first round series. Noren—in what would be the final season of his playing career—led the team with 48 goals and 84 points. Fayetteville's hockey franchise would follow suit after a merger between the Central Hockey League and the Western Professional Hockey League. This new-look CHL would be without the Force's closest rivals meaning an increase in travel and the associated costs. With attendance flagging, those elevated expenses led to the team being folded ahead of the 2001-02 season.

CAPE FEAR FIREANTZ (ACHL; 2002-03)

Professional hockey returned to Fayetteville just one year later with the arrival of the ACHL's Cape Fear FireAntz. Led by head coach Shawn Ulrich—former Asheville Smoke player and coach—the team set up operations in the Crown Coliseum. Ulrich recruited a handful of former Smoke players, including Peter Cermak, Bruce Watson, and Sean Fitzgerald, as well as defenseman Don Martin, who played for the Smoke while they were based out of Brantford, Ontario. Geoff

Derouin—another former Asheville player—split time in goal with former Force netminder Ken Shepard. With their roster set, the FireAntz set out to make their mark.

Their first game, hosting the Knoxville Ice Bears, did little to endear the new squad to Fayetteville's fans. The defense and goaltending looked equally porous, surrendering numerous scoring chances and ten goals against. They promptly followed up with a pair of home wins before losing nine of their next ten contests. The FireAntz' inability to compete on most nights led to Ulrich being replaced behind the bench by Bryan Wells. The one time Thunderbird was met with a level of futility that included ten consecutive losses to end the season.

Cermak did all he could, leading the team in assists (53) and points (74). Fayetteville's offense, aside from the Slovakian winger, was anemic, finishing tied for the second lowest total in the league. The goaltending duo did the best they could, combining for 21 wins and three shutouts, but the team's overall defense finished second worst in the league. The FireAntz failed to qualify for the playoffs, though their average attendance (3,145) trailed only Knoxville, showing that the people of Fayetteville hadn't lost their taste for the game.

CAPE FEAR FIREANTZ (SEHL; 2003-04)

The summer of 2003 brought sweeping changes to the minor league hockey landscape. With the ACHL treading on thin financial ice, David Waronker—who had ownership stakes in four teams—moved his franchises into the newly forged

World Hockey Association 2. The remaining ACHL teams formed the South East Hockey League (SEHL), though the problems were far from over. The Tupelo T-Rex, who played in the Western Professional Hockey League (WPHL) attempted to join the new league, only to be barred by a non-compete contract with the Central Hockey League. With that, the SEHL embarked on an inaugural season that featured just 4 teams:

- Cape Fear FireAntz
- Huntsville Channel Cats
- Knoxville Ice Bears
- Winston-Salem T-Birds

The FireAntz, now under the guidance of head coach Scott Rex, struggled out of the gate and dropped three of their first five games. Despite notable performances from Matt Kohansky (25 goals, 61 points) and David Bagley (28 goals, 60 points), Cape Fear could not gain traction in the standings. That said, they made a brief postseason appearance before being eliminated by Knoxville. Their attendance (2,874 per game) dropped slightly from their lone ACHL season, though it was good enough to place them at the top of the 4-team league. Changes, however, were again on the way.

FAYETTEVILLE FIREANTZ (SPHL; 2004-17)

After completion of the 2003-04 season, the SEHL franchises in Huntsville and Winston-Salem folded, while the remaining teams merged in with the WHA2 to form the Southern Professional Hockey League (SPHL). Dropping the regional precursor, Cape Fear became known as the Fayetteville Fire-Antz. The team replaced Scott Rex ahead of the 2004-05 season, with Derek Booth taking his place as head coach. There was plenty of turnover throughout the lineup, too. Cermak, Watson, and Derouin were all gone, with a new crop of talent recruited in their stead. Steve Roberts, a 30-year-old veteran of several leagues in North American and Great Britain, carried the load offensively with 38 goals and 69 points.

Centers Kory Baker and Tyler Perry also carved out impressive seasons. Baker netted 57 points (14 goals; 43 assists) in just 32 games; Perry added 55 points (16 goals; 39 assists) in 35 games. Chad Collins took up the mantle of number one goaltender with a 25-13 record and four shutouts. The team won six of their last ten games, securing a trip to the playoffs. The appearance was a blink-and-you'll-miss-it affair, as the FireAntz lost a single-elimination matchup against the Columbus Cottonmouths.

Fayetteville performed much the same during the 2005-06 season, finishing in the middle of the league with 68 points. Dean Jackson, in his first full season with the team, led the squad in goals (34) and points (76). Defenseman Mike Clarke had his most productive season by netting nine goals and 67 points, complimented by 103 penalty minutes. Chad Collins, a 24-year-old out of Guelph, Ontario, wasn't the starting goaltender, but he certainly made his case for the job. Appearing in 17 games, Collins won eight; more impressive were his goals against average (2.06), save percentage (.941), and two shutouts.

The FireAntz returned to the playoffs; unfortunately, their previous shortcomings came along with them and they fell to the Florida Seals. Baker tried to will the team to a series win, picking up a goal and four assists while fellow center George Nistas netted four goals. With the exception of game two—in which the entire team suffered a meltdown—Collins was solid in goal, cementing his place as the team's top netminder.

John Marks—who coached the Charlotte Checkers to an ECHL championship a decade earlier—came in to coach the FireAntz ahead of the 2006-07 season and the team responded incredibly well. While the typical ups and downs showed up throughout the season, Fayetteville went on a tear, winning 11 consecutive games from mid-February until mid-March. The team finished second in the league, trailing Columbus by just four points. Even more impressive was the offensive improvement which placed the FireAntz atop the league in goals scored. The team boasted two 30-goal scorers in Tim Velemirovich and B. J. Stephens; Rob Sich fell just short with 29 but did so in only 25 games after coming over in a trade with Florida.

Collins, despite suffering a setback in certain statistics,

thrived as the top goaltender, claiming 27 wins. With strong play at every position, expectations were raised as the team headed into the 2007 playoffs. The FireAntz started strong, quickly eliminating Huntsville before knocking off Knoxville and earning a berth in the finals against the Jacksonville Barracudas. Fayetteville captured the President's Cup in four games, bringing the city its first championship. Sich and winger Josh Welter each put up 15 points while Collins continued his reliable play, earning the title of playoff MVP.

On top of winning the league championship, the FireAntz hit record attendance during the 2007-08 season with over 100,000 fans[1] passing through the Crown Coliseum turnstiles.

Marks departed after the season, returning to coach in the ECHL. Former Florida Seals' head coach Tom Stewart was hired as his replacement, bringing with him a fresh approach to the game. The team played a stronger defensive game, cutting their goals against by seven in 2007-08. Their offense, however, suffered as they scored 60 fewer goals than the year prior. Still, the FireAntz played well enough to return to the playoffs and defend their title.

After rolling over the Richmond Renegades in the opening round, Fayetteville appeared to be ready to make another deep run. The second round matched them up against the Jacksonville Barracudas; in a closely contested game, the FireAntz took the series opener. The second game followed suit, though it was Jacksonville claiming victory. The third and final game got out of hand as the Barracudas netted six goals en route to a series victory. With the goal of winning back-to-back championships dashed, the FireAntz set their sights on next season.

Fayetteville's offense improved in 2008-09, their 214 goals placing them third in goals scored in the SPHL. Sich led the way with 40 goals and 78 points; not content with offense alone, he also racked up 141 penalty minutes, tops on the team. Unfortunately, the defense was not as solid and Collins's play in net suffered. The team again finished third in the league, though their play offered little hope for a better result in the playoffs. As the first round began, it looked like the FireAntz would experience another early offseason.

Matched up against Columbus, Fayetteville surrendered nine goals in the opening game of the series. The porous defense that hindered them during the regular season threatened to cripple them in the postseason. In the second game, the FireAntz put up seven goals, rebounding nicely and drawing even in the series. The teams traded wins as they headed for a decisive game five, in which Fayetteville shut out their opponent. While it had been ugly at times, they had gotten out of the first round.

Because of the configuration of the league, the series victory granted Fayetteville a berth in the President's Cup Finals. Matched up against the defending champion Knoxville Ice Bears, the FireAntz had the opportunity to claim their second championship in three years. They went into game six of the final round with a 3-2 series lead; as the game went into overtime, Fayetteville was one goal away from claiming the title. Instead, Knoxville took the game and the momentum.

The Ice Bears outplayed the FireAntz in game seven, taking home their second consecutive—and third overall—title.

Fayetteville's offense was strong again in 2009-10, scoring a league-high 231 goals. Sich had his best season as a pro, finishing the year with 63 goals and 98 points. His goal-scoring output placed him first in the league, 16 goals higher than the runner-up. The goaltending duo of Guy St. Vincent and Bryan Bridges combined for 31 wins and three shutouts, helping the FireAntz hold on to a playoff spot. It was, however, short-lived, with Fayetteville getting bounced in the opening round.

2010-11 marked a transitional period for the team and bore witness to them struggling throughout the year. Winger Chris Leveille had a solid campaign with 33 goals and 76 points, good enough to lead the team. Sich, despite appearing in only 38 games before being traded to Huntsville, picked up 26 goals and 48 points. Sadly, there wasn't much offense beyond those two, and the team finished in a tie for the third-least amount of goals scored. The FireAntz missed the playoffs for the first time in their existence, which led to Stewart being replaced by Sean Gillam behind the bench during the offseason.

The change in coaches did nothing to spark the team; the FireAntz opened the 2011-12 season with eight losses in their first ten games. They surrendered a league-high 240 goals, a whopping 38 more than the second-worst team. The team's futility led to Gillam's mid-season replacement with Todd Bidner. Sich returned via a trade, but nothing helped to better the team's performance. They finished dead last in the league, missing the postseason for the second year in a row.

The offseason brought another coaching change when Mark DeSantis became the FireAntz' third coach in as many years. The team responded, winning nine of their first ten to open the 2012-13 season. Second year player Josh McQuade had a breakout season, leading the team in goals (42) and points (79). Veteran goaltender Marco Emond enjoyed a banner season with 25 wins and two shutouts, helping the team go from worst in the league to the top of the standings.

The magic failed to carry over from the regular season as Huntsville promptly eliminated Fayetteville, despite finishing 25 points behind the FireAntz in the standings. The disappointment was immense, coming hot on the heels of their best-ever season. DeSantis was named Coach of the Year but moved on to new opportunities during the summer; 31-year-old Greg McCauley became his successor. The team came out of the gates ice cold and dropped their first three contests. In late January 2014, McCauley resigned from his post for personal reasons.

Former player Emery Olauson stepped in behind the bench, inheriting a listless team with a 14-15-0-3 record. Even with a new coach, the team was unable to right the ship as they went 7-15-0-2 over their final 24 games. After the success of the previous season, the FireAntz missed the playoffs and posted the third-worst campaign in their ten-year history. Olauson returned for the 2014-15 season but the team, while showing marginal improvement in the standings, failed to qualify for the postseason yet again.

The team let Olauson go after two subpar seasons, replacing him with longtime CHL player Jeff Bes. Kyle Gibbons paced an improved Fayetteville offense with 31 goals while winger Josh McQuade's 65 points led the team. They scored 24 more goals in 2015-16 than they had the prior season and their goal differential improved to a +22. Parker Van Buskirk was solid in goal with 21 wins and two shutouts. Their improved performance under Bes was good enough to earn them a return to the playoffs after a two-year absence.

The FireAntz started strong, dispatching the Knoxville Ice Bears in the opening round with Van Buskirk earning a shutout in the deciding game. The second round gave them a matchup against the Peoria Rivermen, a series that saw Fayetteville's momentum evaporate along with their offense. It was a shorter appearance than the team would have preferred, but Bes' system promised to keep the FireAntz competitive into the future. Things, however, would prove to be a mixed bag.

The 2016-17 season was a rollercoaster from the opening puck drop. Fayetteville won their first three games before falling into a six game winless streak. They followed this up by winning seven of their next ten. The team heated up as the calendar rolled into 2017 with an eight-game win streak followed closely by a nine-game unbeaten run. True to form, they lost four of their final five games, though they finished second overall in the league.

Fayetteville's offense and defense both improved during

the season; they scored their highest goal total in five seasons while posting the best defensive campaign of their existence. Seven players finished in double digit goal scoring, led by center Jake Hauswirth's 27. Sean Bonar emerged as the Fire-Antz's starting goalie, appearing in 49 games and winning 32 of them. Their second consecutive playoff appearance proved to be brief as they fell to the Pensacola Ice Flyers in the opening round.

FAYETTEVILLE MARKSMEN (SPHL; 2017-PRESENT)

A big change came to the franchise towards the end of the season by way of an ownership change[2]. Chuck Norris—no, not *that* Chuck Norris—purchased the team along with his business partner, Jeff Longo. Longo, who had spent eight years as president of the Charlotte Checkers, reaffirmed the team's commitment to the city. Along with new ownership came a rebranding as the FireAntz became the Marksmen. With the team, ownership, and fanbase reinvigorated, the new-look team was ready to set the league on fire.

Yeah, about that.

The Marksmen brought in Nick Mazzolini to replace Bes, who had moved on to Pensacola. Despite the excitement around the rebranded team, the Marksmen stumbled out of the chocks. Just 11 games into the 2017-18 season—with the team sporting a 3-7-0-1 record—Mazzolini was fired. In his stead came interim coach Ryan Cruthers, who coached just two games, posting a 1-0-1 record. The team then hired Phil

Esposito (no, not *that* Phil Esposito) who—drumroll please—was fired after coaching the Marksmen to a 6-18-0-4 record.

The fourth and final coach of the season was John Bierchen. Much like his predecessors, Bierchen failed to coax a consistent effort out of the team. The Marksmen went 2-13, finishing the season with a league-worst mark of 12-38-3-3. Considering the turmoil on the ice and behind the bench, the fans responded well, as Fayetteville saw an increase of 1,131 spectators per game.

Fayetteville finished the season with the league-worst 144 goals for despite the fact that center Jake Hauswirth ranked third in league scoring with 65 points. Eight goaltenders saw action during the year, none of whom posted winning records. It was a rough season, precisely the kind you would expect from a team in transition.

Prior to the 2018-19 season, the Marksmen hired former Huntsville Havoc goaltender Jesse Kallechy to replace Bierchen as the team's head coach. Joining him as an assistant was former NHLer Peter Worrell. Worrell—a veteran of 391 NHL games—played his final pro season with the Charlotte Checkers during the 2005-06 season. The team responded, accumulating 13 more wins that the year before. They raised their goal scoring by 28 and trimmed their goals against by a whopping 61.

While there was no one offensive standout, the Marksmen boasted a balanced attack with six players registering at least 30 points. The goaltending duo of Dillon Kelley and Nathan Perry accounted for 22 of the team's 25 wins and combined for three shutouts. Their improvement was enough to earn a spot in the playoffs, where they were quickly ousted by the Birmingham Bulls. While their postseason run was short, the Marksmen had shown improvement, and looked to build on it as they moved forward.

With Kallechy back behind the bench, the Marksmen opened the 2019-20 campaign by winning eight of their first ten games. During this run, Fayetteville outscored their opponents by a margin of 35-22, picking up a shutout along the way. Their fiery play continued through the season, leaving them with a 31-6-9 record as the calendar ran into March. As the burgeoning COVID-19 pandemic became more severe, the SPHL shut down operations for the remainder of the season, leaving Fayetteville tied for first place in a campaign that would never be completed.

While the SPHL conducted a limited 2020-21 season, the Marksmen were one of several teams electing not to take part, though they stated their intention to return to play for the 2021-22 campaign.

CHAPTER SEVEN

Landfall

CAROLINA HURRICANES (NHL; 1997-PRESENT)

JUNE 16, 1997.

It could be argued that the birth of the Carolina Hurricanes came when Peter Karmanos sat in on Felix Sabates's Raleigh expansion pitch. Many would cite—and rightfully so —the May 6, 1997 announcement that the Hartford Whalers were moving south. For me, the team truly came into existence when team officials unveiled the logo. This brought the reality home, made it tangible. It gave an identity—if only superficially—to the first major-league team to call Raleigh home.

Ultimately, the team would make the Entertainment and Sports Arena in Raleigh their home ice; the problem was that construction didn't begin until July 22 and the facility wouldn't be ready until the 1999-2000 NHL season. This left the team in limbo, searching for a suitable home rink for the next two seasons. The two most viable options for a temporary home were Fayetteville's Crown Coliseum and the venerable Greensboro Coliseum. An exclusivity agreement with the Fayetteville Force made the former an impossibility. With that, the Hurricanes signed a lease which would allow them to play in Greensboro until the completion of their new arena.

While the Coliseum was a suitable venue for an NHL team, the situation created some unique problems for the Hurricanes. Greensboro hockey fans had lost their AHL Monarchs and faced the proposition of paying higher ticket prices to watch live hockey. The 160-mile round trip from Raleigh proved to be a hindrance for fans coming in from the capital, specifically for games during the week. Also, this was a time when most games started at 7:30 and lasted close to three hours, meaning it could be past midnight before many fans returned home. The convergence of these issues left the Hurricanes with attendance issues that plagued their early years.

With the matter of where they would play settled, Carolina general manager Jim Rutherford set about augmenting his team. He completed handful of trades prior to the start of the 1997-98 season, two of which were especially notable. On June 21, Rutherford made the Hurricanes' first official trade when he sent a first-round pick in the 1997 Entry Draft to the San Jose Sharks for a second-round pick in 1997 and a third-round pick in 1998. The Sharks used the pick they received to select defenseman Scott Hannan, who went on to play in the NHL for 16 seasons.

Carolina used the second-round pick to select Brad DeFauw, a winger who would only appear in nine NHL games. The real magic of the trade was the 1998 third-round pick, which the Hurricanes used to select power forward Erik Cole out of Clarkson University. Longtime fans are well-acquainted with Cole; for those who aren't, don't fret, we'll get to him soon.

Then, on August 25, Rutherford made a move that had much more immediate implications when he acquired veteran winger Gary Roberts and goaltender Trevor Kidd from the Calgary Flames. The cost was center Andrew Cassels and a young goaltender name Jean-Sebastian Giguere. Kidd, a first-round pick in the 1990 Draft, had spent five seasons in Calgary and looked to be a solid goaltending partner for Sean Burke, who moved with the team from Hartford.

In Roberts, the Hurricanes received a player on a mission. Eight rough and tumble seasons with the Flames had taken a physical toll on the veteran, leaving him with nerve damage in his neck. The injury worsened, costing Roberts most of the 1994-95 and 1995-96 seasons before he announced his retirement in the summer of 1996. A few months had passed when Roberts learned about a chiropractic technique that could improve his quality of life and alleviate—at least partially—the effects he was experiencing.

Indeed, the therapy worked well enough to allow Roberts to make a return to the NHL. He approached Calgary GM Al Coates to request a move to an Eastern Conference team in order to reduce the strain of the travel-heavy Western Conference. Shortly thereafter, Coates sent him to the Hurricanes, where he sought to regain his form and restart his career.

To help with fan engagement, the team held an event (dubbed "Fan Jam") at the Greensboro Coliseum where fans could meet players and get autographs. It also marked the debut of the Hurricanes' home and road sweaters. I'll never forget seeing Stu Grimson as I walked onto the arena floor and feeling thankful that I didn't have to go head-to-head with him—his nickname, after all, was "The Grim Reaper." I'll also never forget the free cans of Josta, a Pepsi-produced energy soda. I can't remember if it gave me an energy boost, but I can say that its taste was—unique. Let's just say that it did not surprise me when it disappeared from store shelves two years later.

A DELAYED INTRODUCTION

With the pieces of their inaugural roster in place, the Hurricanes began their first training camp in North Carolina. Head coach Paul Maurice worked to acclimate the new additions to his system, and things looked promising as the team prepared to engage in their exhibition schedule. During this time, the team planned to debut their mascot, a mystical "ice hog" named Stormy. The team tapped Phil Madren to don the costume, a fine choice since Madren had also performed as Monty the Lion, mascot for the Greensboro Monarchs.

The Coliseum lights went down prior to a preseason match against the Detroit Red Wings as one of the arena's Zambonis pulled onto the ice. The cover of the snow tank began opening under the glare of a spotlight as a hog caller—I promise that I'm not making any of this up—worked to lure the mascot out. Smoke flowed dramatically out of the opening —thanks to the use of dry ice—yet Stormy didn't emerge. After a moment, the Zamboni driver backed off the ice, leaving restless fans (myself included) to wonder exactly what had just happened.[1]

As it turns out, putting a person inside an ice resurfacer's snow tank along with dry ice is a bad idea. When that person is wearing a suit that can restrict breathing, things get worse.

Dry ice is composed of frozen carbon dioxide, which goes directly from a solid to a gas. When that happens, it depletes the surrounding oxygen supply, which is exactly what occurred to Madren. Thankfully, medical staff checked on him and got him to a local hospital, where he received a clean bill of health.

THE INAUGURAL SEASON

The Hurricanes got off to a rocky start, dropping their first three games before earning a tie in their fourth. They claimed their first win in an October 10 game against the New Jersey Devils, but wouldn't get a second victory for nearly two weeks. By mid-November, with the team struggling to find consistency, Rutherford sent winger Chris Murray to the Ottawa Senators for defenseman Sean Hill. Hill's physical, defense-first style proved positive, but Carolina continued to falter.

Speedy, Finnish winger Sami Kapanen and big center Keith Primeau did an admirable job in pacing the offense. Roberts, Nelson Emerson, and Jeff O'Neill provided scoring depth, but it wasn't enough. Compounding their troubles was the fact that goaltending was inconsistent. For his part, Kidd played well for his new team, posting the league's sixth-best goals against average (2.17) and sat in a tie for third-best save percentage, stopping 92% of the shots he faced. He must have brought some magic in those glorious checkerboard pads.

Burke was the primary issue. The nine-year NHL veteran was struggling on the ice. The problem proved to be more severe when, in early November, police arrested Burke for attacking his wife.[2] Burke—who skipped an entire season rather than re-sign with the New Jersey Devils—didn't like being number two and being supplanted by Kidd may have acted as a trigger. He felt he should be the number one, no questions asked, and that was that.

Rutherford—faced with the chance to grant Burke's wish and rid himself of a PR nightmare—shipped the goalie (along with winger Geoff Sanderson and defenseman Enrico Ciccone) to the Vancouver Canucks. In return, the Hurricanes received netminder Kirk McLean and winger Martin Gelinas. The trade, however, did little to change Carolina's fortunes and their struggles continued. Gelinas fit in nicely, picking up 12 goals and 26 points in 40 games with the Hurricanes. McLean appeared in just eight games for Carolina before being dealt to the Florida Panthers in an exchange that brought veteran forward Ray Sheppard to North Carolina.

A BOLD MOVE

The Hurricanes made headlines by signing superstar center Sergei Fedorov to a massive offer sheet in late February.[3] Fedorov—embroiled in a contract dispute with the Detroit Red Wings—signed an offer sheet that was tailor made to scare Detroit off. The base salary of the six-year, $38 million pact was only $2 million. However, it included a $14 million signing bonus, meaning the Russian center would be owed $16 million in the first season alone.

The real kicker was that the contract stipulated that the remaining $12 million be divided into yearly installments unless the team reached the conference finals. Were that to occur, the $12 million would have to be paid in one lump sum. At the time, it was very unlikely that the Hurricanes would go that deep in the playoffs, assuming they reached them at all. The Red Wings, however, were the defending Stanley Cup Champions and most observers expected them to make another deep run.

It was doubtful that Red Wings owner Mike Ilitch—founder of the Little Caesars pizza chain—would be deterred by the contract, regardless of its pay structure. This was also during the pre-salary cap era, so the team faced no league-imposed spending limit. The concern on Detroit's end was that, even if they matched the offer, the disgruntled Fedorov would refuse to report to the team.

In the end, Detroit matched the offer and Fedorov stated his intention to re-join the team and win another Cup—which is precisely what happened. Despite their bold move, the Hurricanes came up short in their quest to land a superstar player. I can't help but wonder what might have been if Detroit declined to match the offer but, in the end, it's all just speculation.

By the end of their first season, the Hurricanes sat dead-last in their division, nine points out of a playoff berth. The bigger issue was attendance, not just from a business stand-point, but a media one as well. Sports Illustrated labeled the Hurricanes a "band of hockey hoboes."[4] Anchors at ESPN—

headquartered just 25 minutes from Hartford—openly mocked the Hurricanes at every opportunity.

As a longtime hockey fan and native North Carolinian, it sucked to see the team draw so much derision. The unfortunate truth is that there was no winning option. There was nowhere to play in Raleigh. Fans in Greensboro were reluctant to embrace the team that had displaced the Monarchs, especially knowing the team would be gone in just two years. Fans in Raleigh couldn't reconcile the constant late nights spent on I-40. For better or worse, the Hurricanes had to work with what they had.

Also, for all the negatives, there was a very special moment during the season opener. Team captain Kevin Dineen scored the first goal in Carolina Hurricanes history almost six months after scoring the last goal for the Hartford Whalers. It's also worth noting that he scored both goals against the Tampa Bay Lightning.

A FREE AGENT SPLASH

In the wake of the failed Fedorov offer sheet, Rutherford again went in search of a big name in the summer of 1998. One of the biggest names available was a familiar one from the franchise's time in Hartford: Ron Francis.

Francis, drafted fourth overall by the Whalers in 1981, picked up 821 points in 714 games before they dealt him to the Pittsburgh Penguins in March 1991. The Hartford GM that traded Francis away? Former Greensboro Generals goal-tender Eddie Johnston.

Small world.

Francis would win back-to-back Stanley Cups in Pittsburgh, racking up 613 points while sharing the ice with the likes of Mario Lemieux and Jaromir Jagr.

Following the 1997-98 season, the Penguins were in a state of transition: Lemieux retired at the end of the 1996-97 season (though he would mount a comeback in late 2000) and, while Jagr remained, the surrounding talent was in need of an over-haul. With this in mind, they allowed the 35-year-old Francis to hit the open market; when he did, Rutherford came calling. Carolina's GM knew what adding the veteran playmaker would do for the team, both on and off the ice, and signed Francis to a four-year contract.[5]

1998-99

All things considered, the Carolina Hurricanes' first season went about as well as one could reasonably expect. To ensure that the second would go smoother, the team needed a reliable goalie to split time with Kidd. Rutherford addressed this by signing veteran Arturs Irbe[6] to a one-year contract. The Latvian-born Irbe—who had become a folk hero during his time with the San Jose Sharks—was coming off of one-year stints with the Dallas Stars and Vancouver Canucks.

The league shook up its alignment, moving from four divisions to six. The Hurricanes landed in the new Southeast Division, alongside the Florida Panthers, Tampa Bay Lightning, and Washington Capitals. Just as it had during their first season, it took five games to see the team claim its first victory of the campaign, a 3-1 win over Vancouver. They did, however, find a higher level of consistency this time around and shot to the top of their division.

Seeking to help his team's offense and spark an ailing power play, Rutherford made a deal that sent Emerson to the Chicago Blackhawks. In return, Carolina landed Paul Coffey[7], the second-highest scoring defenseman in NHL history. This marked Coffey's second stint with the franchise, as he spent 20 games with the team during the 1996-97 season, their last in Hartford. Despite the veteran defender's sluggish output (two goals and eight assists in 44 games), the Hurricanes saw overall offensive improvement, though their power play regressed.

For the first time in five years, Irbe appeared in over 50 games, seeing action in 62 contests for Carolina. His play proved steady enough to earn the starting job and the man affectionately known as "Archie" rewarded his team by finishing in the top-ten for goals against average, save percentage, shutouts, and wins. More importantly, his convincing performance played a big part in the Hurricanes claiming their first postseason berth.

Their opponent came in the form of a Boston Bruins team that boasted future Hall of Famer Ray Bourque, second-year center Joe Thornton, and leading scorer Jason Allison. Buoyed by this trio and with strong goaltending from Byron Dafoe, the Bruins eliminated the Hurricanes in six games. Irbe's reliable play from the regular season continued, but—outside of Sheppard's five goals—Boston stymied Carolina's offense. Even with the sting of a first-round exit, there was hope for the future after the improvement shown in year two. Unfortunately, the team soon suffered an enormous loss.

Following the game six loss, the Hurricanes flew back to Raleigh, landing sometime around 1 AM; a handful of players then drove to Roberts' house for a get-together. After a few hours, taxis were called to take them home, however, only one arrived.[8] While they waited for the additional cars to show, defenseman Steve Chiasson opted to drive himself home. This decision proved fateful as, shortly after 4 AM, Chiasson was involved in a single-car accident and succumbed to his injuries.

The death of Chiasson—a highly regarded teammate—deeply impacted the Hurricanes and, more importantly, left a void in the lives of his wife and children.

"It's a very painful time for all of us."
-Carolina Hurricanes coach Paul Maurice

To commemorate Chiasson and his impact on the team, the Hurricanes established the Steve Chiasson Award, given annually to the player "who best exemplifies determination and dedication while proving to be an inspiration to his teammates through his performance and approach to the game."

The players select the winner at the conclusion of each season, with the inaugural award going to Sean Hill.

1999-2000

As the Hurricanes fought through the loss of their teammate, they faced two major changes. One was positive; the other negative and a threat to the core of the team.

The 1999-2000 season would mark the team's first in the Entertainment and Sports Arena, their new state-of-the-art facility in Raleigh. Gone were the days of 90 minute drives to "home" games, replaced by the stability of settling into their new home rink. There was excitement aplenty, for both the players and for the fans. There was, however, a dark cloud that emerged and threw the team's immediate future into doubt.

Primeau, the team's captain and leading scorer in each of their first two seasons, needed a new contract. Talks between the center and the team had been ongoing since the summer, though an agreement never came to pass. For Primeau, the main sticking point was maintaining his unrestricted free agent status in the future[9], something that Carolina's offers would have hampered.

As the stalemate stretched on, Rutherford negotiated several trades, though each one fell through. The one that came closest to fruition would have seen the Hurricanes send Primeau to the Phoenix Coyotes as part of a package for goal-scoring winger Keith Tkachuk. Karmanos—when asked why the trade failed to materialize—pointed to Tkachuk's contract, which jumped from $4.3 million for the 1999-2000 season to $8.3 million in 2000-2001. While Tkachuk had twice hit the 50-goal mark, that salary was almost unthinkable at the time. As a result, Karmanos was as eager to avoid it as the Coyotes were to unload it.

Despite the drama, the Hurricanes opened the new campaign with back-to-back wins on the road. They finally played a game in their new home on October 29, a 4-2 loss to the New Jersey Devils. From there, the team stumbled into the new year, suffering a five-game losing streak in mid-January. They followed this up with a 4-1 victory over Buffalo on January 22, but still sat with a record of 18-22-8-0.

The following day, the Primeau saga finally drew to a close when Rutherford sent the disgruntled center to the Philadelphia Flyers along with a fifth round pick. In return, the Hurricanes received center Rod Brind'Amour, goaltender Jean-Marc Pelletier, and a second-round pick. The distraction was over, allowing the team to move forward.

Brind'Amour—the centerpiece of Carolina's return—played his first game with his new team on January 24, a 3-2 overtime victory over the Montreal Canadiens. While he didn't register a point, the new acquisition acquitted himself well, playing a hard-nosed, physical game through 21 minutes of ice time. The center's work ethic sparked the team to a 19-13-2-0 mark over the 34 games following his arrival. It wasn't perfect, but it was an improvement.

Still, the team only mustered a third-place finish in their division, missing the playoffs by a single point.

2000-2001

The Hurricanes made a series of moves ahead of the 2000-2001 season; the most promising was the acquisition of offensive defenseman Sandis Ozolinsh from the Colorado Avalanche. At 28 and coming off a 16 goal, 52 point campaign, Rutherford expected Ozolinsh to bolster Carolina's blueline offense and spark their power play.

The team again struggled with consistency, trading wins and losses. Their longest winning streak was four games, a mark that they hit only once. Both their offense and defense fared worse than the season before, though their special teams did show improvement. O'Neill eclipsed the 40-goal mark, leading the team with 41 while Francis paced the team with 50 assists. The team also benefitted from improved scoring depth, with Brind'Amour, Kapanen, and Gelinas hitting at or above 20 goals.

In his first full season, winger Shane Willis—bolstered by a booming slapshot—put up 20 goals and 44 points in 73 games. Ozolinsh netted 12 goals and 44 points, including 19 points on the man advantage. Second-year defender David Tanabe added 29 points in 74 games, while Glen Wesley and Marek Malik each broke 20-points. Veteran Kevin Hatcher—signed during the summer—brought a steady, defense-first game in what would be his final NHL season.

For the third consecutive year, Irbe handled the majority of goaltending duties. Appearing in a career-high 77 games, Irbe notched 37 wins and six shutouts, earning himself votes for both the Hart Memorial Trophy (NHL MVP) and Vezina (Top Goaltender). Backup duties fell to Tyler Moss, who amassed a 1-6 record in 12 appearances. While Irbe's performance spoke for itself, the play of his backups since arriving in Carolina led to him taking on a massive workload. Over his first three seasons with the Hurricanes, Irbe appeared in all but 32 of Carolina's 246 games.

The Hurricanes qualified for the playoffs as the eighth seed in the Eastern Conference. Unfortunately, this gave them a first-round matchup against a powerhouse New Jersey team that finished 23 points up on Carolina during the regular season. That gap was apparent early as the Devils won the first three games by a combined score of 9-1. Carolina won a pair of 3-2 contests to draw back to within a game of tying the series before a 5-1 thrashing in game six ended the series and sent the Hurricanes home early.

New Jersey's stifling defense—bolstered by the goaltending of Martin Brodeur—proved insurmountable for the Hurricanes. In fact, it propelled the Devils all the way to game seven of the Stanley Cup Final, where they ultimately fell to the Colorado Avalanche.

Though the season ended prematurely, it marked the first appearance for two longtime roster mainstays: center Josef Vasicek and defenseman Niclas Wallin.

2001-2002

Not content with his team, Rutherford set to work in the summer of 2001. His first move saw him sent a fifth round pick to Colorado in return for hulking winger Chris Dingman. Two weeks later, he sent a second round pick to Detroit for defenseman Aaron Ward. These two moves amped up the team's toughness and added two players with Stanley Cup championships on their resumes. Rutherford furthered this experience when he signed veteran goaltender (and two-time Stanley Cup winner) Tom Barrasso to split time with Irbe.

Another new addition was rookie winger Erik Cole, drafted by the Hurricanes in 1998 with a pick gained in the team's first ever trade.

The team came out of the gates strong; the offense showed signs of life and Irbe provided the reliable net minding that fans had come to expect. Unfortunately, the inconsistency that plagued the team in years prior returned, leaving them unable to build any momentum. In early December, Rutherford completed a trade to bring Sean Hill—who signed with the St. Louis Blues during the summer of 2000—back into the fold. The team responded by winning seven of their next ten games.

Then, they won just three out of their next eight. Something was missing, and the GM set to work addressing it. He traded Ozolinsh, whose game slipped during his time in Raleigh, and forward Byron Ritchie to Florida for a package including center Kevyn Adams and smooth-skating defenseman Bret Hedican[10].

The team responded with just a single win through the ten games following the trade. Things continued largely unchanged into early March when Rutherford, not content with the performance of his goaltenders, sent Dingman and Willis to Tampa for goalie Kevin Weekes. It was a sad turn of events for Willis, whose career was derailed after suffering a concussion at the hands of New Jersey's Scott Stevens in the second game of the 2001 playoffs. After missing the rest of the postseason, Willis returned to the Hurricanes lineup only to suffer another concussion after receiving an elbow from San Jose defender Bryan Marchment[11] in November 2001.

Weekes appeared in just two regular season games, but made enough of an impression that Rutherford felt comfortable sending Barrasso to Toronto for a fourth round pick. With the playoffs approaching, the Hurricanes would roll with the tandem of Irbe and Weekes.

PRIMED FOR A DEEP RUN

By the end of the season, Carolina sat atop their division, despite showing only marginal improvement. The hockey gods rewarded them with another first-round matchup against the New Jersey Devils and their All-Star goalie. This time, however, it was the Hurricanes who took control. The "BBC Line," consisting of Brind'Amour, Cole, and Bates Battaglia, took over the series, with the trio combining for four goals and three assists in the series.

Irbe was solid early, stopping 64 of 66 shots through

games one and two. The shift to New Jersey's Continental Airlines Arena for game three was a different matter. Already up 2-0, the Devils struck again less than a minute into the second period, leading head coach Paul Maurice to pull Irbe in favor of Weekes. The young goalie stopped 22 of 23 shots, but the Hurricanes were unable to solve Brodeur, dropping the game by a score of 4-0.

Maurice tapped Irbe to start game four, only to see his starter suffer the same fate. After surrendering two goals on eight shots, Weekes went in and performed well. Still, Carolina could only beat Brodeur once, and New Jersey held on to tie the series at two games apiece.

Weekes got the nod for game five, his first ever NHL post-season start. To be blunt, Weekes was brilliant. With the teams battling to a 2-2 tie at the end of regulation, the pressure was on and the 27-year-old netminder rose to the challenge. The defining moment of the series came early in overtime when Weekes stopped a shot from New Jersey's Stephane Richer. The rebound popped into the slot as Weekes lay prone on the ice.

Devil's center John Madden—undoubtedly tasting a 3-2 series lead—fired the loose puck towards the unguarded net. In a moment that Hurricanes fans will never forget, Weekes stretched out in desperation, his glove snaring the puck and keeping his team alive. Madden stood in shocked disbelief as Weekes casually skated away with the play blown dead.

With momentum from the game-saving stop, the Hurricanes pressed the attack; Josef Vasicek put the game-winning goal home and Carolina went into game six with the chance to close out the series. Weekes made his second consecutive start in what became another goaltending duel. Ron Francis netted a power play goal midway through the second period, a marker that wound up being the series clincher. Weekes turned aside 32 New Jersey shots, earning himself a shutout and the Hurricanes a trip to the second round.

The Montreal Canadiens were coming off of their best season in four years heading into the 2002 playoffs. Better yet, they upended their arch nemesis, the Boston Bruins, in the opening round. Despite the lack of a superstar player, Montreal got by with offensive depth and clutch goaltending from Jose Theodore. The 25-year-old Quebec native was in peak form, coming off a regular season performance that netted him both the Hart and Vezina trophies.

With mounting confidence, Carolina took game one as Weekes picked up another shutout, though his play soon dipped. After losing the next two games and yielding two goals on nine shots in game four, Weekes ceded the crease to Irbe. The change worked. The Latvian netminder held his own until Wallin—beginning his reputation as "The Secret Weapon"—won the game in overtime.

Irbe stayed in net for games five and six; the Hurricanes won both by a combined score of 13-3. The team and its goalies had shown resilience and were rewarded by a spot in the Eastern Conference Finals opposite another Original Six franchise from Canada: the Toronto Maple Leafs.

The teams traded 2-1 victories, with Wallin scoring his

second overtime winner of the postseason. Irbe continued matching Toronto's Curtis Joseph in game three, another overtime affair. Not wanting Wallin to have all the fun, Jeff O'Neill picked up the game winner, giving Carolina a 2-1 victory. The ice in game four was tilted in favor of the Maple Leafs, who outshot the Hurricanes 31-15. Despite this, Carolina beat Joseph three times while Irbe stopped every shot he faced, and the Hurricanes took a 3-1 series lead.

With their backs against the wall, Toronto managed just 19 shots in game five. A power play goal late in the first period was all the Leafs needed, as Joseph responded with a shutout of his own. This set the table for a make or break game six at the Air Canada Centre in Toronto, with the home team looking to force a winner-take-all game seven.

A packed house in Toronto watched as the teams fought tooth and nail to gain the upper hand. For the Maple Leafs, it was win or be eliminated. For the Hurricanes, it was the chance to reach the Stanley Cup Final for the first time in franchise history. The implications were enormous.

For over 50 minutes, the teams traded scoring opportunities, including five power plays apiece. Irbe and Joseph held their ground, turning aside shot after shot, some in spectacular fashion. Finally, just past the halfway mark of the third period, Jeff O'Neill forced Toronto defenseman Tomas Kaberle into a turnover, giving the Carolina winger a clear path to the net. Joseph made the initial save, only to have the puck carry over him and fall into the crease. Slowing down as he approached the net front, O'Neill scooped the puck into the open goal, giving the Hurricanes a 1-0 lead.

As time wound down, Toronto's desperation rose. It was clear that Irbe would stop any shot he could see, so the Maple Leafs did their best to flood the slot with traffic. Finally, with less than a minute remaining and the Toronto net empty, captain Mats Sundin poked a loose puck past a sprawling Irbe, tying the game.

With five overtime victories under their playoff belts, the Hurricanes were confident they would emerge victorious. In spite of this, it was Toronto who came out with the early pressure, leaving Carolina scrambling. With their goaltender holding the fort, the Hurricanes were able to stabilize and build their game. Their heavy forecheck became stifling, ultimately leading to the series-winning goal.

As the clock ticked down towards 12 minutes, Martin Gelinas dumped the puck into Toronto's zone. Defender Anders Eriksson—pressured by Carolina's Jaroslav Svoboda—played the puck back to Maple Leaf winger Alex Mogilny, who tried to rifle it around the boards behind his own net. The positioning of Eriksson and Svoboda forced Mogilny to alter his angle on the fly, leading to a weak attempt which Josef Vasicek intercepted. The big center turned toward the net, where both Svoboda and Gelinas had skated, and fired a pass. Despite Mogilny's efforts to tie him up, Gelinas was able to tip the puck past a sprawling Joseph.

The Carolina Hurricanes were the Eastern Conference

champions and now had their sights set on capturing hockey's ultimate prize.

FIRST TRIP TO THE STANLEY CUP FINAL

In what seemed a surreal event to many in the hockey world, the Hurricanes battled their way to the final round of the Stanley Cup Playoffs. Despite the adversity they had faced, their greatest challenge came in the Detroit Red Wings. Having won the second of their back-to-back championships just four years prior, the Red Wings boasted a stable of All-Stars. Their forward corps included Steve Yzerman, Sergei Fedorov, Brendan Shanahan, Brett Hull, Luc Robitaille, and a young Pavel Datsyuk. Their defense contained a wealth of skilled veterans, headed by one of the all-time greats in Nicklas Lidstrom.

As if that roster wasn't impressive enough, Detroit had arguably the best goalie of his generation in Dominik Hasek. After utilizing Mike Vernon and Chris Osgood for championships in 1997 and 1998, the Red Wings acquired Hasek in the summer of 2001 to cement one of the greatest rosters assembled in NHL history.

But, as the old saying goes, games are won on the ice. The Hurricanes were well aware of the opposition and the fact that winning the series would require every ounce of determination they could muster.

For a moment, it looked like they might just pull it off.

The teams scrapped their way to a 2-2 tie, sending the first game of the series into overtime. The fans in Detroit barely had time to settle back into their seats for the extra period before the Hurricanes closed out the game. After causing a turnover behind the goal line, O'Neill fed the puck to Francis, who stood unopposed in front of the Red Wing net. Carolina's captain tipped the shot past Hasek, stunning the crowd and showing that this team still had some fight left.

Detroit struck back, claiming a 3-1 victory in game two and setting the stage for what would be the defining game of the postseason. With the series shifting to Raleigh for game three, the teams once again traded goals and stretched the game past regulation time. Both teams traded volleys through one overtime period, then two. Each team failed to convert on a power play in the second overtime as fatigue began setting in.

The third overtime period gave the teams renewed vigor and the game more action. Irbe and Hasek went save-for-save as the clock dipped under the six-minute mark. Then, on the final rush of the game, Igor Larionov—a veteran of 12 NHL seasons—weaved through Carolina's defense and flipped a backhand shot past a scrambling Irbe, giving the Red Wings a 2-1 series lead. Detroit went on to outscore the Hurricanes 6-1 in games four and five, capturing the Stanley Cup and ending Carolina's magical postseason run.

THE HANGOVER

The 2002-03 season saw the Hurricanes stumble badly from the heights of their flirtation with Lord Stanley's Cup. The issues came hard and fast, hindering the team's offense, defense, and special teams. In an attempt to inject some life into the struggling squad, Rutherford acquired winger Jan Hlavac from the Vancouver Canucks. Hlavac, who posted a 28-goal campaign just two years prior, had suffered a notable setback in his play. This, unfortunately, carried over to his stint in Carolina, and he could not regain his goal-scoring touch.

When the new campaign started, the Hurricanes struggled to tread water, suffering consecutive shutouts to end 2002. They suffered two extended losing streaks, managing just two wins in 18 games from January to mid-February. As it became apparent another playoff appearance had slipped away, Rutherford began moving out veterans: he sent Kapanen to Philadelphia, Wesley to Toronto, and Battaglia to Colorado.

There was also a changing of the guard in net as Weekes supplanted Irbe as the starting goaltender. Though the team played poorly, Weekes played very well, accounting for nearly two-thirds of Carolina's wins and posting five shutouts. Irbe, on the other hand, was regressing, picking up just seven wins in 34 appearances.

O'Neill and Francis paced the offense, with both players having successful seasons and being the only players to hit the 20-goal mark. Brind'Amour and Cole were effective when healthy, but the pair missed a combined 63 games due to injuries. By year's end, the team sat dead last in the NHL and faced serious issues around their on-ice performance.

Rutherford made several moves during the offseason, most notably adding defensemen Danny Markov and Bob Boughner. With lingering concern over Irbe's performance, he also signed Jamie Storr—a former seventh overall pick of the Los Angeles Kings—to a one-year contract.

The 2003-04 campaign saw another poor start as Carolina didn't claim their first victory until the fifth game of the season. Weekes continued his steady play and Irbe showed improvement. Still, the team managed just five wins in their first 20 games. Offensively, there was a production decline across the board and—for the first time since relocating—no one on the roster reached 20 goals.

In December, with the team holding an 8-12-8-2 record, Rutherford fired head coach Paul Maurice and replaced him with former New York Islanders coach Peter Laviolette. The Hurricanes responded with stronger play, though it wasn't enough to earn a return to the playoffs. More moves followed as Markov—almost exactly seven months after becoming a Hurricane—was sent to Philadelphia in exchange for a young winger named Justin Williams.

You'll want to remember that name.

The last move of the season came at the trade deadline when captain Ron Francis was moved to Toronto in exchange for a fourth round pick. This gave the veteran, who had brought credibility to the fledgling franchise, a final shot at winning another Stanley Cup.

This season also marked the NHL debut of center Eric Staal. The second overall pick at the 2003 Entry Draft, Staal appeared in 81 games for Carolina, posting 11 goals and 20 assists. The team held high hopes for the lanky center from Thunder Bay, Ontario native. However, another year would pass before he got the chance to really show what he could do.

THE DRAFT COMES TO RALEIGH

Two years after their first Stanley Cup Final appearance, the Hurricanes hosted the 2004 NHL Entry Draft. Not only did this put the focus of the hockey world on Raleigh again, but fans would have the opportunity to witness the selection of the league's future stars. Washington selected Russian phenom Alexander Ovechkin with the first overall pick. Pittsburgh followed, taking center Evgeni Malkin with the second pick.

After Chicago's selection of Medicine Hat Tigers' defenseman Cam Barker, NHL Commissioner Gary Bettman notified the crowd that there was a trade to announce. Carolina sent their first-round pick (eighth overall) and second round pick to Columbus in exchange for the fourth overall selection. With the pick, Rutherford selected Calgary Hitmen winger Andrew Ladd, a talented and physical player who accumulated 286 penalty minutes over his final two seasons of junior hockey.

There was excitement among the fanbase, though something brewed below the surface that threatened to delay the debuts of the newly drafted players.

THE LOST SEASON

As the NHL's collective bargaining—signed to end the 1994 lockout—expired, the league met with the NHL Players' Association (NHLPA) to hammer out a new deal. On September 16, 2004—one day after the previous agreement expired—the league initiated a lockout. At first, there were hopes that the two sides would reach a deal quickly, allowing for a 2004-05 season with minimal loss of games. With talks gaining no ground, weeks bled into months, and that optimism evaporated.

The primary sticking point was on what commissioner Gary Bettman called "cost certainty." The league floated the idea of a luxury tax during the 1994 lockout. This "tax" would be levied against teams based on player salaries above league average. The NHLPA rebuffed this proposal, countering that revenue sharing was a better means to achieve the league's financial goals.

During the 2004-05 lockout, the focus was on implementing a salary cap. This became a major point of contention between the two sides as talks dragged on. I won't delve much deeper into this, aside from saying that the dispute eventually led to the cancellation of the 2004-05 season. This marked the first time that a major sports league in North America lost an entire season because of an ongoing labor dispute. The sides finally reached an agreement in July 2005, one that included a $39 million salary cap for the 2005-06 season, as well as revenue sharing.

There were several changes to the game as well, the most publicized (and controversial) being the addition of the shootout. In the event teams remained tied after a five minute, three-on-three overtime, a shootout would be the deciding factor. Other rule changes included eliminating two-line passes, shrinking the neutral zone by four feet, and a reduction in the allowable size of goaltender equipment. These changes —as well as a few others—were implemented with the goal of increasing offense and improving the flow of the game.

With the lockout business settled, Rutherford set about retooling his team.

A NEW ERA

Carolina's GM didn't let the offseason distractions hold up his business. Before the start of the lockout, he shipped longtime starter Irbe to the Columbus Blue Jackets for future considerations. This marked the end of Irbe's NHL career, as he would never suit up in another league game. To help fill the void, Rutherford sent defenseman Tomas Malec to the Mighty Ducks of Anaheim in return for goaltender Martin Gerber. Coming off of two solid seasons as a backup in Anaheim, the Swiss-born Gerber wanted a shot at the number one spot.

He brought in rugged defender Mike Commodore from the Calgary Flames, adding size and physicality to the blue-line. Franchise mainstay Jeff O'Neill departed via a trade to the Toronto Maple Leafs. A first-round pick of the Hartford Whalers, O'Neil scored 176 goals in 536 games for the Hurricanes. While losing the winger hurt Carolina's offense, Ruther-ford made a pair of moves to make up the difference.

He signed ten-year NHLer Cory Stillman, one year removed from hoisting the Stanley Cup with the Tampa Bay Lightning—a championship in which they defeated Commodore's Flames in seven games. The 2003-04 campaign was a career best for the winger, seeing him rack up 25 goals and 80 points in 81 games. Along with his offensive prowess, Stillman brought leadership and a championship pedigree.

Rutherford also signed 13-year vet Ray Whitney, a jour-neyman with solid offensive capability. After breaking in with the San Jose Sharks—along with Arturs Irbe—Whitney had stops in Edmonton, Florida, Columbus, and Detroit before landing in Carolina. The signings of Stillman and Whitney gave the Hurricanes a pair of underrated players, each capable of being major contributors. With the roster set, the Hurri-canes set their sights on returning to the playoffs.

The season opened inauspiciously with a 5-2 loss to the Lightning in Tampa. Gerber struggled, ceding the net to rookie goaltender Cam Ward after surrendering four goals on 19 shots. Ward, unfazed by Tampa's attack, stopped 10 out of 11 shots, showing flashes of what he was capable of. The first glimpse of Ward's potential came in the Hurricanes' home opener two nights later.

Their opponent: the Pittsburgh Penguins.

Despite a roster featuring NHL legend Mario Lemieux and rookie phenom Sidney Crosby, the Penguins were a strug-gling franchise. Three seasons near the bottom of the league culminated with Pittsburgh winning the 2005 NHL Draft Lottery, enabling them to select Crosby with the first overall pick. While they boasted one of the game's best-ever players and a rookie poised to make history, Pittsburgh's roster had yet to be fully fleshed out.

With Gerber nursing an injured hip, Laviolette tapped Ward for his first NHL start. If the pressure of facing such lauded talent rattled him, the Saskatoon, Saskatchewan native didn't show it. Staal and Stillman put Carolina up 2-0, a lead they held into the third period. Tallies from Pittsburgh's Ryan Malone and Ziggy Palffy evened the score and gave the fans in Raleigh their first taste of the league's revamped overtime setup.

The excitement ramped up as overtime gave way to the shootout, and all eyes were on Ward. With nothing less than ice water coursing through his veins, the rookie turned aside Lemieux and Palffy, preserving Stillman's goal for Carolina. Pittsburgh's last chance came from Crosby; unfortunately for the Penguins, Ward was up to the task, shutting the door and securing Carolina's first win of the season.

As weeks turned into months, the Hurricanes sat atop their division while earning a reputation as one of the Eastern Conference's best teams. Rutherford, seeing that the team he assembled had potential for a long postseason run, sought to add veteran depth. On January 30, 2006, he acquired center Doug Weight from the St. Louis Blues. With 13 seasons under his belt, Weight was seeking to add a Stanley Cup championship to his impressive resume. His new team continued their strong play into early March, when the team suffered the loss of one of their key contributors.

During a March 4 game against the Penguins—a bout the Hurricanes would eventually win by a score of 7-5—Pittsburgh defenseman Brooks Orpik drove Erik Cole into the boards headfirst. The hit earned Orpik 17 minutes in penalties —including a game misconduct—while leaving Cole with two fractured vertebrae. At the time, the power forward had 29 goals and 30 assists in 60 games. Now, after nearly being paralyzed, Cole's hockey future was in limbo. With 22 games remaining in the season, the Hurricanes had a large hole to fill.

Sure enough, Rutherford got to work again.

On March 9, Carolina brought in Mark Recchi from the very team that Cole suffered his injury against. Recchi, who was a part of Pittsburgh's 1991 Championship, brought offensive depth and leadership to a team that was starting to fully realize their potential. The lineup adjustments weren't seamless, seeing Carolina go 9-11 over their final 20 games and losing the Conference's top spot to the Ottawa Senators. Still, there were bright spots for the team as they prepared for the 2006 Stanley Cup Playoffs.

Gerber set a new franchise record by recording 38 wins for Carolina. Staal—in just his second season—scored 45 goals and 100 points. Justin Williams, in his first full season with the Hurricanes, set new career highs in goals (31), assists (45), and points (76). Stillman and Whitney—two largely unheralded free agent signings—combined for 38 goals and 131 points. Despite this, there was reason for concern as the post-season began.

WHATEVER IT TAKES

For Carolina, the 2006 playoffs opened against a Montreal Canadiens team that finished 19 points below them in the standings. On paper, Montreal were the underdogs. That illusion shattered once the series began. The Canadiens won the opening game 6-1 before taking game two in overtime. Following the most successful season in team history, the Hurricanes were heading to Montreal in desperate need of a win. To achieve that, they turned to a new starting goaltender.

Ward, who relieved Gerber early in game two, got the nod for his first NHL playoff start. The rookie was brilliant, standing on his head to keep his team in the game. At the other end, Huet Carolina's newcomer save for save. The teams again headed to overtime with the Hurricanes trying to avoid an 0-3 deficit. Eric Staal provided, giving Carolina a victory and a shot of adrenaline.

Laviolette stayed with Ward for the rest of the series, and the former Red Deer Rebel didn't disappoint. The calm and composed Ward stopped 78 out of 82 shots, helping the Hurricanes close out the series in six games. Carolina bent without breaking and survived the first round; now, they would face a familiar postseason foe in the New Jersey Devils. Adding to the intrigue were the divergent paths that each team had taken.

The Devils closed out their regular season with an 11-game winning streak before completing a sweep of the New York Rangers. Over their final 11 games, the Hurricanes went 5-4-2 and struggled early in their opening series before righting the ship. For many, the focus went to the goaltending matchup. New Jersey's Martin Brodeur—a three-time Stanley Cup winner—versus Ward, a rookie who grew up idolizing his series opponent.

The Hurricanes came out flying and rolled to a 6-0 victory in game one, setting the table for a memorable game two. New Jersey center Scott Gomez gave the Devils a 2-1 lead with 21 seconds remaining in the third period. A Carolina flurry followed, ending with Staal tying the game three seconds before the horn. Then, just over three minutes into overtime, Wallin beat Brodeur on a partial break, flexing his prowess for scoring huge playoff goals. Despite a hiccup in game four—during which Ward yielded the net temporarily back to Gerber—the Hurricanes overpowered the Devils and closed out the series in five games.

For the second time in four years, the Hurricanes reached the Eastern Conference Final, drawing a matchup with the Buffalo Sabres. With both teams employing a fast-paced style and just two points separating their regular season finish, the series promised to be evenly matched. As the series opened, it was Buffalo that controlled play. Ward's play faltered slightly, opening the door for Gerber to regain the net. The change worked, albeit briefly, as the Swiss netminder shut the Sabres out in the fourth game of the series.

Ward returned to the crease in game five after Gerber allowed three goals and held Buffalo off the scoresheet for the rest of the game. The Hurricanes held on to win, taking a 3-2 lead in the series. The Sabres responded with a 2-1 overtime victory in game six to force a decisive seventh game. Buffalo carried a 2-1 lead into the third period, but goals from Weight, Brind'Amour, and Williams secured a 4-2 Carolina victory and a return to the Stanley Cup Final.

The Edmonton Oilers entered the 2006 Stanley Cup Playoffs as the eighth seed in the Western Conference. The franchise, five-time Cup winners, were making their first appearance in the final series since their last championship in 1990. Along their path, they eliminated the league-leading Detroit Red Wings, the San Jose Sharks, and the Mighty Ducks of Anaheim. As the series got underway, the Oilers showed no signs of slowing down.

Skating to a 3-0 lead early in the second period of game one, Edmonton was in full control. Then—at 17:17, naturally —Brind'Amour pounced on a rebound and slammed the puck past goaltender Dwayne Roloson. Carolina turned up the pressure in the third, and was rewarded with goals from Whitney and Williams. The Oilers battled back to tie the game, only to suffer a major blow when defenseman Marc-Andre Bergeron checked Carolina forward Andrew Ladd into Roloson. The netminder—who provided outstanding goaltending throughout the playoffs—left with an injured knee.

He would not return in the series, a shame since he was arguably Edmonton's MVP during the postseason.

Backup goalie Ty Conklin entered the game as each team vied for the go-ahead goal. With the clock ticking below the one minute mark, overtime seemed like an inevitability. Following a neutral zone face-off, the Hurricanes fired the puck into Edmonton's zone, drawing Conklin out to play it behind his net. Intending to leave the puck for Oilers' captain Jason Smith, Conklin turned away. Smith attempted to move the puck, only to find Brind'Amour breathing down his neck.

Carolina's captain took the loose puck and wrapped a backhanded shot into the vacant net. It was an exciting—if unexpected—end to the first game. As the series progressed, Edmonton turned to goaltender Jussi Markkanen and, while he played well, he could not slow the Hurricanes. The series returned to Raleigh for game five, with Carolina holding a 3-1 lead. This presented a prime opportunity for the team to capture the first Stanley Cup in franchise history in front of a raucous home crowd. As overtime began, Edmonton's Steve Staios went off for tripping, putting the Hurricanes on the power play.

The electricity in the air could have powered Raleigh for a month. This team, picked by experts to be bottom-dwellers, stood poised to become league champions. Rutherford's savvy moves, Brind'Amour's leadership by example, and Ward's emergence brought North Carolina to the brink of its first major-league title; all it would take was one goal on the man advantage. The standing room only crowd roared, awaiting the inevitable glory.

With the Hurricanes trying to break out of their own end,

Cory Stillman received a pass from Staal along the boards. As Staal skated toward the blue line, Stillman sent a soft return pass that Fernando Pisani intercepted. In alone on the rookie goaltender, the Edmonton winger fired a shot that beat Ward's glove, just inside the far post. The game was over. The Stanley Cup remained in its case, the fans left stunned, and the loss forced the Hurricanes to move on to game six in Alberta.

Compounding their stunning loss, the Hurricanes would be without Doug Weight, who suffered a shoulder injury early in the third period of game five. A boost would come in the form of Erik Cole, who returned to Carolina's lineup after missing three months while recovering from his neck injury. However, the Oilers rode the momentum of their overtime victory to a dominant performance in front of their fans. Propelled by three power play goals, they claimed a 4-0 win and forced a seventh game in Raleigh.

Another standing-room crowd watched as the Hurricanes went on the attack. Aaron Ward fired a shot past Markkanen at 1:26 of the first period, sending the packed house into a frenzy. Frantisek Kaberle put home his fourth goal of the play-offs to put Carolina up 2-0, a lead they held going into the third period.

An Edmonton flurry ended when Pisani lifted the puck past Ward and cut the Hurricanes' lead in half. The score held steady until late in the period when the Oilers—who pulled Markkanen for an extra attacker—won an offensive zone face-off. A deflected pass sent the puck to the boards, where Hedican batted it forward. Eric Staal gathered it and fired a pass to a streaking Justin Williams, who shot it into the empty net and sealed a 3-1 Carolina victory.

While the series was certainly closer than the Hurricanes would have liked, they came out on top. Cam Ward received the Conn Smythe Trophy, becoming the first rookie goaltender to win the Stanley Cup and playoff MVP honors since Patrick Roy in Montreal twenty years prior. The most enduring image of Carolina's championship came when Brind'Amour took the Stanley Cup and hoisted it overhead, brimming with emotion after winning the ultimate prize in his sixteenth season.

The Hurricanes were on top of the hockey world; unfortunately, the good times wouldn't last.

THE HANGOVER, PART TWO

Following their Stanley Cup victory, the Hurricanes underwent a number of roster changes. Mark Recchi and Doug Weight—both brought in to bolster the lineup for the playoffs —returned to their former teams; Recchi to Pittsburg, Weight to St. Louis. Matt Cullen departed Raleigh for the New York Rangers. Martin Gerber, who Ward supplanted as the go to goalie, signed on with the Ottawa Senators. To fill the backup spot, Rutherford signed veteran netminder John Grahame to a two-year pact.

The GM completed a handful of trades to round out the roster prior to the season. After spending the first five seasons of his career with the Hurricanes, Josef Vasicek was traded to

Nashville in exchange for winger Scott Walker. Jack Johnson —Carolina's first-round pick in 2005—was packaged and sent to Los Angeles; in return, the Hurricanes received defenseman Tim Gleason and center Eric Belanger. With the team in place, Carolina set off to defend their league title, though it quickly became apparent that something was off.

The Hurricanes began the season with four consecutive losses before stringing together three wins. Their inconsistent play continued, leaving the team with a 21-16-4 record as the calendar rolled into 2007. More trades came in the hopes of sparking the team. Kevyn Adams went to Phoenix for defenseman Dennis Seidenberg. Belanger was sent to Nashville in a move that brought Vasicek back to Carolina. Winger Anson Carter was acquired from Columbus for a fifth-round pick, but failed to click with the team, netting one goal in ten appearances.

Despite the moves, the Hurricanes failed to qualify for postseason play. In doing so, they became the first team in a decade to follow up a championship by not making the playoffs.

Prior to the start of the 2007-08 season, few changes were made to the Hurricanes' roster. Of the notable offseason moves, Cullen was re-acquired from New York while Michael Leighton came in to add goaltending depth. Rutherford brought in burly winger Wade Brookbank to add toughness to the lineup. Unfortunately, the inconsistency continued. Their offense showed improvement, though team defense took a hit.

Subpar goaltending compounded the issue. Both Grahame

and Leighton struggled, leading the team to lean heavily on their starter. Appearing in 69 games, Ward picked up 37 wins and four shutouts. His reliable play was a bonus, though a steady backup would have gone a long way toward improving Carolina's record.

On January 8, 2008, the team claimed former first-round pick Sergei Samsonov off waivers from the Chicago Blackhawks. Samsonov—a member of the Oilers squad that fell to Carolina in 2006—racked up 14 goals and 32 points in just 38 games with the Hurricanes. On February 11, Rutherford sent Cory Stillman and Mike Commodore to Ottawa for defenseman Joe Corvo and winger Patrick Eaves. Then, at the February 26 trade deadline, Rutherford traded Andrew Ladd to Chicago for Finnish forward Tuomo Ruutu.

Ruutu—a 2001 first-round pick of the Blackhawks—was struggling to reach his potential, hindered by injuries. Ladd found himself in a similar situation with the Hurricanes, so a change of scenery for the two seemed reasonable. Ruutu appeared in 17 games for Carolina following the trade, picking up four goals and 11 points.

Despite Ward's 37 wins, the Hurricanes went into their last game of the season needing a win to return to the playoffs. Following a decisive win over the Tampa Bay Lightning, there was reason to believe the Hurricanes could grind out another victory with their season on the line. Instead, the visiting Florida Panthers won a 4-3 contest and left Carolina on the outside once again as the postseason began.

FALSE HOPE

After two seasons without reaching the playoffs, the team needed a spark. To address this, fan favorite Erik Cole was dealt to the Edmonton Oilers. Coming back was slick-skating offensive defenseman Joni Pitkanen. While trading a beloved player can be a risky endeavor, the Hurricanes opened the 2008-09 season with consecutive wins, showing promise that they had righted the ship. However, they followed this by winning just five of their next ten games, scoring just one goal in three of those contests.

On December 3, 2008, with the team continuing to struggle, Rutherford fired Peter Laviolette. While he had recently become the winningest American-born coach in NHL history, Carolina's GM felt the team's chemistry needed a change[12]. Rutherford didn't have to look far, tapping former Hurricanes' coach Paul Maurice as the replacement. Maurice spent the previous two seasons as bench boss in Toronto, winning 76 out of 164 games and missing the playoffs in both campaigns.

The team was slow to respond, losing four of their first five games after Maurice's return. Following a five-game losing streak in January 2009, the team started to find their footing. In early February, Rutherford traded for versatile forward Jussi Jokinen. He made two more moves in March, first sending Justin Williams to Los Angeles for Patrick O'Sullivan, who was then traded to Edmonton to re-acquire Eric Cole.

Following Cole's return, the Hurricanes went 12-3-2 to finish the season. Thanks to this, they earned a trip to the playoffs as the sixth seed in the Eastern Conference. For their troubles, Carolina earned another postseason matchup against the New Jersey Devils. Through the first six games, both teams traded wins, forcing the series to a seventh game at New Jersey's Prudential Center. The Devil's held a 3-2 lead deep into the third period; with their season on the line, the Hurricanes hemmed New Jersey into their own zone.

The puck nearly exited the zone when a pass from Brind'Amour trickled towards the blueline. Tim Gleason dropped to his knees, corralling the puck and moving it to Pitkanen, who then executed a cross-ice pass. Jokinen fired a shot into the net, tying the game and giving the Hurricanes life. Beyond that, it left the Devils and their fans reeling. It turned to shock when, with 31.7 seconds remaining, Eric Staal rifled a wrist shot past Martin Brodeur and gave Carolina a 4-3 lead.

New Jersey scrambled to tie the game, only to have Ward and the Hurricanes hold on for the win. Besting the Devils gave Carolina the opportunity to face the top seed in the East. The Boston Bruins finished 19 points ahead of Carolina during the regular season. The disparity was evident early on, as Boston claimed a 4-1 victory in the opening game. Carolina didn't stay down, answering with a convincing performance and a 3-0 win in game two. They went on to win the next two games and take a 3-1 series lead, outscoring the Bruins 7-3.

As the series returned to Boston's TD Banknorth Garden, the Bruins showed the form that carried them to the league's second-best record during the regular season. They dominated play, outshooting Carolina and skating to a 4-0 win. The game wasn't without controversy as, late in the third period, former Hurricane Aaron Ward got into a shoving match with Matt Cullen. Scott Walker skated in and struck Ward with an ungloved punch, sending the defenseman to the ice. A scrum ensued, after which Walker received 17 minutes in penalties, including a ten-minute misconduct.

The misconduct carried an automatic suspension, a punishment that the league rescinded. As a result, Walker was left with just a $2,500 fine, an outcome that didn't sit well with the Bruins.

"I just didn't like what happened. I just don't think there was any need for that. He dropped his gloves and sucker-punched him[13]."

Claude Julien, Boston Head Coach

Boston used the incident as motivation and—with phenomenal goaltending from Tim Thomas—took game six by a score of 4-2. For the Hurricanes, it was another seventh game on the road, this time for a berth in the Eastern Conference Final. As the puck dropped, the teams went to war, neither ceding much ground and, as the third period dwindled away, the game was deadlocked and destined for overtime. Each team had chances to wrap up the series during the extra frame, though both goaltenders held firm.

The chances continued, though as time fell below the two-minute mark, it seemed that a single overtime period wouldn't be sufficient. Then, with the puck in the neutral zone, Dennis Seidenberg fed a pass to Ray Whitney, who carried it into Boston's zone and fired a shot from the top of the face-off circle. Thomas bobbled the rebound, allowing Scott Walker—who else—to bat the puck into the net. In the blink of an eye, the Hurricanes eliminated the top seed in the conference and secured a trip to the third round.

Their opponent would be the Sidney Crosby-led Pittsburgh Penguins, a team looking for their second consecutive appearance in the league's final series. The previous year, Pittsburgh lost in the championship round to the Detroit Red Wings. That experience, coupled with the one-two punch of Crosby and Malkin down the middle, proved too much for the Hurricanes to overcome, and they fell in four games.

The unceremonious end to their postseason return stung, but things were about to get much worse.

THE DROUGHT

Despite making a run to the Conference Finals, there was a sense of flux around the Hurricanes as they entered the summer of 2009. Rutherford made a series of moves to beef up his defense, signing free agents Jay Harrison and Andrew Alberts as well as re-acquiring Aaron Ward via trade. He also boosted the team's forward depth with the signings of two-time Stanley Cup champion Stephane Yelle and rugged winger Tom Kostopoulos.

Any excitement about the new season burned away quickly. If dropping their first two games—while being outscored 9-2—was the kindling, suffering a 14-game losing streak was the gasoline. The team signed veteran netminder Manny Legace to stabilize the backup position, though the team continued their futility. In early December, Rutherford traded Philippe Paradis less than six months after selecting him in the first round of the 2009 Entry Draft. In return, Carolina received forward Jiri Tlusty from the Toronto Maple Leafs.

No matter the changes, the team's inconsistent play persisted. Once it became clear that the Hurricanes would not qualify for the postseason, a flurry of moves took place. Niclas Wallin, Matt Cullen, Scott Walker, Joe Corvo, Aaron Ward, Alberts, and Yelle were all traded away. In their stead came a collection of draft picks that didn't pan out and players who made minimal impacts on the team.

The biggest shift came from a change in leadership. Brind'Amour struggled through a season that was well below his standard, eventually ceding the captaincy to Staal. The move did little to inspire the team, though it drew ire from segments of the fanbase. Another culture-altering event occurred after the season when Brind'Amour announced his retirement after 20 years, half of which he spent in Carolina.

The team saw an 11-point improvement in 2010-11, though this wasn't enough to earn a playoff appearance. There was a bright spot, as first-year wing Jeff Skinner burst onto the scene with a 31-goal, 63-point campaign and captured the Calder Trophy as the league's most outstanding rookie. Staal, Ruutu, Cole, and Jokinen all gave strong performances as did Corvo, who put up 40 points from the blueline. Cam Ward was reliable as ever, picking up 37 wins and four shutouts, though it was clear the team lacked the supporting cast to get them over the hump.

In late January, the Hurricanes and the city of Raleigh became the center of the hockey world's attention when the RBC Center played host to the 2011 NHL All-Star Game. Carolina boasted three players at the event: center Eric Staal, winger Jeff Skinner, and goaltender Cam Ward. Defenseman Jamie McBain also represented the team in the Super Skills Competition as a rookie.

The 2011-12 season marked another setback for the Hurricanes, seeing them fall to a fifth place finish in the Southeast Division. Jokinen, Skinner, and Ruutu all suffered reduced offensive output; compounding this was Cole's departure during the offseason, wounding the team's shallow depth. Ward again did everything he could, racking up five shutouts and the fifth 30-win season of his career. Carolina's slow start led to another casualty when Maurice was fired following an 8-13-4 start. Nineteen-year NHL veteran Kirk Muller became the new head coach and, while the team's performance showed some improvement, they still experienced an early start to the offseason.

With a new coach in place, Rutherford set his sights on

improving the roster. He made quite a splash on day one of the 2012 NHL Draft when he acquired Jordan Staal from Pittsburgh and signed the center to a ten-year, $60 million contract. In a bid to further bolster the forward corps, Rutherford signed winger Alexander Semin to a one-year, $7 million pact. The signing faced heavy scrutiny as the offensive-minded Semin was coming off two years of decreased production and questions surrounding his commitment and work ethic. The promise of him regaining his scoring touch certainly made it an interesting gamble.

While NHL GMs tweaked their rosters to prepare for the season, trouble brewed behind the scenes. The Collective Bargaining Agreement which ended the 2004-05 lockout expired on September 16, 2012, and did so without a new pact in place. With the players and owners at a stalemate, the league faced its third lockout in 19 years and just seven years after losing an entire season. Weeks bled into months before the league ratified a new CBA on January 6, 2013. This allowed the league to embark on a 48-game schedule starting on January 19.

Unfortunately, the Hurricanes would start the season without Ruutu, as offseason hip surgery sidelined the forward for all but 17 games. Cam Ward suffered a strained MCL in early March, robbing Carolina of their starting goalie. Despite these setbacks, the team showed signs of improvement. When Justin Peters shut out the Washington Capitals on March 12, Carolina appeared to be trending in the right direction.

However, when the teams met again two days later, it was

Washington claiming victory. The loss bewildered the Hurricanes and marked the beginning of a seven-game losing streak. They enjoyed a brief respite—a 3-1 victory over Winnipeg—before suffering another seven-game winless stretch.

Then, during an April 2 match against the Capitals, the Hurricanes defenseman Joni Pitkanen. Pitkanen—attempting to beat out an icing call—went into the end boards awkwardly and had to be taken off on a stretcher. The frightening collision left him with a severely broken heel, an injury that ultimately marked the end of Pitkanen's NHL career.

The season concluded with the fourth straight spring with no playoff hockey in Raleigh.

Despite the tribulations and disappointing end, the season offered a sentimental moment for the Staal family. For the final game of the year, the team called up Jared, the youngest of the Staal brothers, from Charlotte. For the opening face-off, he lined up with Eric and Jordan; the only Staal missing was Marc, a defenseman for the visiting New York Rangers, who missed the game because of an eye injury.

Now, let's go back to the signing of Alex Semin.

The mercurial winger had a strong first season with the Hurricanes, putting up 13 goals and 44 points in 44 games. His performance earned him a five-year, $35 million contract extension, signed during a prolonged losing streak for the team.

Several personnel moves occurred prior to the 2013-14 season. Nathan Gerbe—coming off of five seasons with the Buffalo Sabres—came in to add speed to the team's top nine.

Veterans Radek Dvorak and Manny Malhotra added depth up front. The chance to play in the NHL was especially significant to Malhotra. After suffering an eye injury while playing for the Vancouver Canucks, doctors declared Malhotra medically unfit to play.

Undeterred, Malhotra signed a professional tryout contract with the AHL Charlotte Checkers. After eight games in the Queen City, the Hurricanes signed the veteran center to a one-year contract. Rutherford also made additions to the blueline, signing Ron Hainsey and trading for Andrej Sekera. Finally, goaltender Anton Khudobin came in to share duties with Cam Ward.

There were also major changes to the layout of the league. A new four division format was implemented, taking the Hurricanes out of the Southeast Division and placing them into the new Metropolitan Division.

Metropolitan Division
Carolina Hurricanes
Columbus Blue Jackets
New Jersey Devils
New York Islanders
New York Rangers
Philadelphia Flyers
Pittsburgh Penguins
Washington Capitals

The Hurricanes showed improvement but, overall, their

inconsistency continued haunting them. Compounding this was the loss of both Khudobin and Ward to injuries within the first month of the season. Justin Peters became the de facto starter and performed admirably, but it was clear that—to have success—Carolina would need their injured netminders to return.

The team—desperate for help—signed former New York Islanders goalie (and first overall pick from the 2000 draft) Rick DiPietro to a tryout contract with their AHL affiliate in Charlotte. The experiment was short-lived as the Checkers released the Lewiston, Maine native, after he posted an 0-4 record.

Ward would be the first to return, stopping 26 of 29 shots in a 4-1 loss to the Boston Bruins in mid-November. Over his next ten starts, the Albertan goalie went 4-6 and posted a save percentage at 90 percent or better just twice. The team struggled to find their footing and slipped out of playoff contention, at least for the moment.

On New Year's Day, Rutherford traded Gleason to Toronto; in return, Carolina received two-way defenseman John-Michael Liles and collegiate defender Dennis Robertson. Liles, who scored ten or more goals four times while a member of the Colorado Avalanche, never reached those heights in Toronto and looked to rebound with the Hurricanes. In their final trade of the season, the team sent Ruutu to New Jersey after spending parts of seven seasons in Raleigh.

The beginning of the new year also marked Khudobin's return to the lineup and a jolt to the Hurricanes' results. The

Kazakh-born goaltender won his first four starts, single-handedly stealing games for Carolina. His heroics, however, weren't enough to save the team's season, as they finished ten points out of the playoffs. One could imagine how the team would have fared if not for the goaltending injuries they suffered early on.

Following another disappointing campaign, the Hurricanes underwent major changes. Two weeks after season's end, Rutherford stepped aside as General Manager; Ron Francis was named as his replacement. The first official move of his tenure was firing head coach Kirk Muller and replacing him with former Detroit Red Wings assistant coach Bill Peters.

Aside from the front office and coaching shakeup, the summer was uneventful. Veteran center Jay McClement came in on a one-year contract, as did Tim Gleason, returning after a brief stint with Toronto.

With a new bench boss and new GM, there was hope for better results on the ice. As it played out, the 2014-15 campaign saw the same inconsistent—often listless—Hurricanes drop their first eight games. The team was in complete disarray, being outscored 33-15; they either scored a few goals and got subpar net minding or got a solid performance in net while generating no offense.

Goaltending again came down to Ward and Khudobin and, while Ward rebounded statistically, Khudobin's play noticeably dropped. In 34 appearances, he managed just eight wins, while Ward picked up 22 victories in 50 games. However, the goalies were not the only downfall for Carolina.

The season prior, the Hurricanes ranked 23rd in goals scored with 207. During Peters' first year, the team lit the lamp just 188 times and Eric Staal was the only player to crack the 20-goal mark, finishing the season with 23 tallies. Skinner, in his fifth season, suffered a 15-goal drop-off from the year before, despite appearing in six more games. The biggest disappointment came from Alex Semin, in just the second year of his five-year contract.

To be fair, the mercurial winger never seemed to mesh with his new coach, resulting in Semin watching many games from the press box. When he did see action, he was ineffective, finishing with just six goals in 57 games. While his play certainly underwhelmed, one has to wonder how much the clashes with Peters hindered his performance. Regardless of where you stand on the issue, the Hurricanes needed much more out of Semin than what they got.

Outside of their season-opening skid, Carolina suffered losing streaks of three or more games eight times during the year. While the power play and penalty kill showed some improvement, missed opportunities outweighed them. As a result, the Hurricanes finished 27 points out of a playoff spot, marking the sixth consecutive season that they failed to reach the postseason.

Dark times indeed.

Francis acted proactively during the offseason, starting with his goaltending. He shipped Khudobin to the Anaheim Ducks for defenseman James Wisniewski and trading two draft picks to the Vancouver Canucks in exchange for Swedish goaltender Eddie Lack. Lack, 28, showed promise in Vancouver while splitting time first with Roberto Luongo and then Ryan Miller; the Canucks, however, wanted to make room for the up-and-coming Jacob Markstrom.

The sophomore GM then acquired Kris Versteeg—a two-time Stanley Cup winner—from the Chicago Blackhawks. Rounding out the roster changes were four rookies: defensemen Noah Hanifin, Brett Pesce, and Jaccob Slavin, along with forward Brock McGinn. Finally, Francis bought out the remainder of Semin's contract, marking an abrupt end to the talented—yet inconsistent—forward's time in Raleigh.

The pieces were in place as the opening night of the 2015-16 season approached. Then—as if an omen—less than four minutes into their first game, Wisniewski suffered a season-ending injury against the Nashville Predators. The Hurricanes went on to lose their first three games and claimed just four wins in their first ten outings. With the same culprits—anemic offense, inconsistent goaltending—plaguing the team, it was clear that the foundation needed to be rebuilt.

THE NEXT GENERATION

Francis began by trading veterans Versteeg and Liles, collecting draft picks and prospects in return. The biggest move came when he moved Eric Staal to the New York Rangers on February 28, 2016. The trade didn't come as a surprise, considering Staal's decline in play (ten goals through 63 games) and expiring contract. Still, it marked the end of an era as the team drafted and developed Staal, who became the face of the team. It also left Cam Ward as the last remaining member of the 2006 Stanley Cup team.

The summer brought further changes: Wisniewski—who never played another shift for Carolina after his injury—had his contract bought out. The team added veteran forwards Lee Stempniak and Viktor Stalberg to the roster, though the biggest move came in a trade with the Chicago Blackhawks. After capturing three Stanley Cups in a six-season span, Chicago needed to shed salary, and Ron Francis was willing to help.

For a price.

With that in mind, the Blackhawks sent winger Bryan Bickell and the remaining $4 million of his contract to the Hurricanes for two draft picks. The price Chicago paid to unload Bickell's contract was 21-year-old Finnish winger Teuvo Teravainen. Francis added another young Finn to the mix when he signed Sebastian Aho, a second round pick from 2015, to an entry-level contract. Aho and Teravainen—along with Elias Lindholm and Victor Rask—gave the Hurricanes a crop of promising young forwards on their revamped roster.

The 2016-17 season began much the same way as the prior one; Carolina lost their first three games and won just three of their first ten. There was, however, promise, as the team's youth rose to the forefront. Team scoring was led by Skinner (24-years-old), Aho (19), and Rask (23), while Lindholm (22), Teravainen (22), Justin Faulk (24), and Jaccob Slavin (22) finished in the top-ten.

Even with the positives, the team continued struggling, allowing ten more goals than the year before. Both Ward and Lack performed close to their 2015-16 levels, though each showed the tendency to allow soft goals. This culminated in early March when Peters called out Lack and urged him to "make a save."

The coach also used a colorful adjective, one that I won't print here, but I'm sure you can guess what it was. Likewise, I'm sure you can guess how the season ended: no playoffs.

A storyline, one much bigger than the game itself, emerged in early November when Bryan Bickell received a multiple sclerosis diagnosis. Bickell had been dealing with various issues since his time in Chicago: fatigue, unexplained aches, and dizziness. At times, doctors believed he was suffering from vertigo, though treatments to address it gave him no relief. Further testing revealed lesions on Bickell's brain and spinal cord, leading to the discovery of the true culprit.

To better understand what to expect, Bickell reached out to former NHL goaltender Josh Harding, who was diagnosed with MS in 2012. He began a treatment regime aimed to ease the symptoms, though there was uncertainty about his future on and off the ice. Eventually, Bickell began working out again, a change that helped his mental wellbeing. He returned to the team in April and played in each of the final four games of the season.

The Hurricanes closed the season out against the Philadelphia Flyers, the team Bickell's Blackhawks defeated to win the 2010 Stanley Cup. The teams played to a 3-3 tie, neither team was able to break through in overtime. When Jordan Weal could not beat Eddie Lack, Bickell was announced as Carolina's first shooter. He skated in and fired a wrist shot from the top of the slot that beat Philadelphia goaltender Anthony Stolarz cleanly. Carolina's bench erupted in celebration, cheering on their teammate.

The Hurricanes went on to win 4-3.

With his return triumphant, Bickell announced his retirement on October 4, 2017, after signing a one-day contract with the Blackhawks.

Rewinding to January 2017, the franchise garnered attention when TSN's Pierre LeBrun spoke with Peter Karmanos. The owner, then 73, spoke candidly about his willingness to sell the team either outright or in part[14]. This ignited speculation surrounding the team's future, including the possibility of relocation (again). Then, in August, word came out that Karmanos agreed to a term sheet with Chuck Greenberg, former CEO of Major League Baseball's Texas Rangers. The press release indicated that the sale would be worth approximately $500 million and, while this didn't represent a purchase agreement, it showed that Karmanos was willing to listen to offers.

As the uncertainty of the team's future loomed large, Francis spent the summer of 2017 seeking goaltending help and, for a time, it looked like he found it.

The Blackhawks—yes, them again—had an established starter in Corey Crawford, but, when he suffered an injury during the 2015 playoffs, it pressed backup Scott Darling into action. Despite having no NHL playoff experience, Darling led the Blackhawks past the Nashville Predators in the opening round. Crawford returned and led the Blackhawks to a championship, but Darling had already cemented himself as a folk hero in Chicago.

Through three seasons with the Blackhawks, Darling posted strong numbers, which made him an attractive target for a General Manager in search of a potential starter. On April 28, 2017, Francis pounced, sending a third round pick to Chicago for the goalie before signing him to a four-year, $16.6 million contract. Two months later, Francis sent Lack to Calgary, cementing Darling and Ward as the team's netminding tandem.

Former Hurricane Justin Williams returned to Raleigh after signing a two-year contract. Williams spent the prior two seasons with the Washington Capitals after winning two Stanley Cups with the Los Angeles Kings. Another former player re-signed, though under different circumstances. Following a 13-year career —nine of which were spent with Carolina—Erik Cole signed a ceremonial contract, allowing him to retire as a Hurricane.

When the business of playing hockey commenced, it was —again—more of the same. The biggest sign of hope was the chemistry that developed between Aho and Teravainen, as both players set career-highs in 2017-18. Slavin and Pesce also continued establishing themselves as Carolina's defensive cornerstones.

Still, there were issues plaguing the team.

The offense improved, though goaltending again proved to be a sore spot. Darling, brought in to take over starting duties, faltered badly during his first season with Carolina, posting just 13 wins in 43 appearances. His struggles led to Ward getting more starts, and the veteran responded admirably with 23 wins and a better save percentage and goals against average than his platoon mate.

There were still major questions surrounding the franchise, the biggest of which had nothing to do with the team's performance. Karmanos' negotiations with Greenberg failed to advance, leaving the door open for other parties to put in offers to purchase the team.

A NEW ERA

One such offer came from Texas businessman Tom Dundon, who made his interest known in late 2017. Unlike Greenberg's offer, negotiations moved along at a brisk pace and, on January 11, 2018, Dundon purchased 52 percent of the team —along with the operating rights to PNC Arena—for $420 million.

For the first time since moving to North Carolina, the Hurricanes had a new majority owner. Dundon immediately asserted himself as a hands-on owner, someone who wouldn't be content to sit idly by. As the new owner settled in, the Hurricanes forged on as best they could. From the time of the sale through the end of the season, they posted a record of 17-

20-3, finishing out of the playoffs for the ninth consecutive year.

This didn't sit well with Dundon, and changes were made which reflected that.

Three weeks after their last game, Francis had his contract terminated. A month prior, he was moved out of the GM position and named president of hockey operations. Don Waddell—who joined the franchise in 2014—took over as interim general manager. Waddell, who served in management roles with the Detroit Red Wings and Atlanta Thrashers, brought a wealth of knowledge into his new role.

Another change followed soon after, as Peters resigned as head coach, exercising an "out clause" in his contract. Dundon and Waddell immediately set off in search of Peters' replacement.

In the end, they didn't have to look far.

On May 8, 2018, the team named former Hurricane Rod Brind'Amour as their new head coach. The next step was tweaking the roster with the goal of ending the playoff drought and returning the team to prominence. On the second day of the 2018 draft, Waddell traded Elias Lindholm and Noah Hanifin to the Calgary Flames. In return, Carolina received offensive defenseman Dougie Hamilton, rugged winger Micheal Ferland, and the rights to defenseman Adam Fox. This marked Waddell's second trade after acquiring forward Jordan Martinook from the Arizona Coyotes on May 3.

Longtime goaltender Cam Ward departed, signing a one-year contract with the Chicago Blackhawks on July 1. Waddell signed free agent netminder Petr Mrazek to split time with Darling. Darling spent the summer working on his conditioning, hoping to regain his form and reestablishing himself in the league.

Waddell continued tinkering with his roster, adding defenseman Calvin de Haan and trading Jeff Skinner to the Buffalo Sabres.

The 2018-19 season approached with a renewed sense of hope. Brind'Amour's system looked good in the preseason, with the team compiling a 5-1 record. They suffered a setback when Darling left with an injury during the team's last exhibition game, an overtime loss to the Nashville Predators. In three preseason appearances, the Virginia-born goalie stopped 61 of 65 shots. Two days later, the Hurricanes—in need of goaltending depth—claimed veteran Curtis McElhinney off of waivers from Toronto.

As the regular season began, it became clear that this Carolina team was different. They relied on forechecking, and did so relentlessly. There were still lapses as the team grew accustomed to their coach's system but, as the season wore on, their talent rose to the fore. Aho broke out with a 30 goal, 83 point campaign; Teravainen added 55 assists and 76 points. Rookie winger Andrei Svechnikov—drafted second overall in 2018—netted 20 goals.

Hamilton chipped in 18 goals, the most by a defenseman in Hurricanes' history. Slavin and Pesce, the team's defensive workhorses, contributed 31 and 29 points, respectively.

Perhaps paramount was the fact that the team got consistent goaltending throughout the season. Mrazek picked up 23 wins and four shutouts in 40 appearances; McElhinney added 20 wins and two shutouts in 33 games played.

Darling, unfortunately, never displayed the renewed play he showed before being injured. The team placed on waivers in November 2018 and subsequently sent him down to the Charlotte Checkers.

Waddell made one major mid-season trade, acquiring Nino Niederreiter in exchange for the slumping Victor Rask. It proved to be a shrewd move as the Swiss forward fit in seamlessly, netting 14 goals and 30 points in 36 games.

The new iteration of the Hurricanes also began a new tradition. Following a home win, the team skated to center ice for a Skol clap. Afterwards, they would engage in a small activity; early on, it involved skating to the end boards and launching themselves against the glass. As the season wore on, the celebrations became more intricate, including spins on bowling, basketball, and boxing, the latter featuring an appearance from former heavyweight champ Evander Holyfield. For the most part, the fans embraced it. Outside of the fanbase, there were plenty of people voicing their displeasure with what they viewed as a minor league gimmick.

One such naysayer was hockey analyst and noted curmudgeon Don Cherry. During a mid-February broadcast of Hockey Night in Canada, Cherry referred to the Hurricanes as —among other things—a bunch of jerks. While he didn't realize it at the time, he had not only contributed to the spectacle; he had given it a tagline. Within two weeks, the team had merchandise emblazoned with the slogan.

The Hurricanes continued rolling and—in their second-to-last game of the season—clinched a playoff berth with a victory over the New Jersey Devils. After the win, Mrazek's excitement boiled over as he exclaimed "We're in" during a post-game interview. It's a moment etched in Hurricanes history as the decade-long postseason dry spell finally came to an end. They rode an emotional high into the playoffs, something they would need to harness to get past their first round opponent: the defending champion Washington Capitals.

Early on, it appeared the Hurricanes were outclassed, dropping the first two games in the nation's capital. Returning to their home ice gave the team a much-needed boost. While they cruised to a 5-0 victory, they lost their skilled rookie when Svechnikov reluctantly dropped the gloves with Washington's star, Alex Ovechkin. The brawl put Carolina's winger in concussion protocol and out of the lineup indefinitely.

Even without the talented Russian, the Hurricanes claimed victory in game four, evening the series at two games apiece. The squads traded wins in the next two games, setting the stage for a winner-take-all game seven in Washington. The Capitals struck early, building leads of 2-0 and 3-1 before Teravainen brought Carolina to within one late in the second. Jordan Staal tied the game early in the third, the last goal that would be scored for over 45 minutes.

The teams battled through one overtime period; Mrazek held strong in Carolina's net, as did Holtby in Washington's.

Speed gave way to physicality, which eventually gave way to fatigue as 80 minutes of game time burned away. By the start of the second overtime, the teams focused on controlling the puck and minimizing mistakes.

For half of the period, that's all there was.

The Hurricanes began mounting pressure, led by Williams —who had developed a reputation as a big-game performer. A face-off in Washington's defensive zone led to a scramble with the puck ending up in the right wing corner. Williams retrieved it, turned, and fired it toward the net, where Brock McGinn tipped it past Holtby and ended the series.

Their second round opponent was the New York Islanders. Led by young center Mathew Barzal and Vezina finalist Robin Lehner in net, the Islanders were coming off their best season in 35 years. It promised to be a tight series, as New York finished the season as the league's top defensive team; Carolina finished sixth in that category, allowing 223 goals versus New York's 196. The opening game of the series lived up to expectations with the Hurricanes claiming a 1-0 victory in overtime.

Game two provided much of the same, though this time the Islanders carried a 1-0 lead into the third period. Carolina's Warren Foegele tied things up just 17 seconds in, giving his team the needed boost to press for offense. Forty-eight seconds later, former Islanders first round pick Nino Niederreiter scored the eventual game winner, and the series shifted to Raleigh with the Hurricanes up 2-0. They went on to sweep the Islanders, claiming games three and four by a combined score of 10-4.

Despite the magic they showed throughout the season and into the playoffs, the Hurricanes could not overcome the Boston Bruins. In a reversal of their second round series, Carolina dropped four consecutive games and missed an opportunity to reach the Stanley Cup Final for the third time. Still, after a decade of futility, the Hurricanes finally appeared to be moving in the right direction.

Waddell—seeing the progress the team was making—continued adding to the roster. McElhinney, who performed well for the Hurricanes, signed with the Tampa Bay Lightning, leaving an opening for Mrazek's backup. With an opportunity to fill that spot and shed salary, he traded Scott Darling to the Florida Panthers; in return, Carolina received goaltender James Reimer.

Adam Fox, the young defenseman acquired from Calgary the year before, was shipped to the New York Rangers after failing to come to an agreement with the Hurricanes. It was a well-known secret that Fox wanted to play for the Rangers, a gamble that Waddell took. While Fox didn't sign in Carolina, the Hurricanes did acquire a pair of draft picks when he was sent to New York.

The GM then picked up a first round pick, a seventh round pick, and center Patrick Marleau from the Toronto Maple Leafs, all for a sixth round pick. Toronto needed to move salary and Waddell was happy to oblige, especially when the payoff was a first round selection. Marleau, however, never suited up for Carolina. He hoped to return to the San Jose Sharks, the team he spent 20 years with. As such, the Hurricanes bought out his contract, making him a free agent.

Calvin de Haan—after just one season of the four-year contract he signed with Carolina—was traded along with young forward Aleksi Saarela to Chicago. Coming to the Hurricanes were defenseman Gustav Forsling and goaltender Anton Forsberg, giving the team added depth. Waddell followed this up by acquiring forward Erik Haula from the Vegas Golden Knights, adding another offensive weapon to his young team. He also added speedy winger Ryan Dzingel, who was coming off of a short stint with the Columbus Blue Jackets.

He also made a splash in the free agent market when he signed offensive defenseman Jake Gardiner to a four-year pact. Gardiner, who fell out of favor in Toronto, gave the Hurricanes another talented blueliner, though it created a logjam. With Faulk, Hamilton, and now Gardiner, it felt inevitable that another move was coming.

In the end, longtime Hurricane Justin Faulk became the odd man out. After eight seasons in Raleigh, Waddell traded him to the St. Louis Blues; Carolina received defenseman Joel Edmundson, a physical, defense-first player. They also received Dominik Bokk, St. Louis' first-round pick from the 2018 draft.

August saw the end of an era in Hurricanes' history. After 14 NHL seasons—all but one with Carolina—Cam Ward signed a one-day contract to retire as a Hurricane. The Alberta native left an indelible mark on the franchise after leading the team to the 2006 Stanley Cup and being named playoff MVP. Ward holds team records for games played (668), wins (318), and shutouts (27).

There was also drama over the summer, courtesy of the Montreal Canadiens. On July 1, Montreal general manager Marc Bergevin signed Sebastian Aho to a five-year offer sheet. The Hurricanes had seven days to either match the offer or decline. In case of the latter, Carolina would receive a first, second, and third round pick from Montreal. Don Waddell, knowing what an important piece Aho was to the team, immediately made it known that the Hurricanes would match.

As fate would have it, Carolina opened the 2019-20 season at home against Montreal. The Hurricanes won 4-3; sadly, Aho did not register a point. While Brind'Amour's team showed occasional growing pains, it was clear that they were trending in the right direction. Aho, Teravainen, and Svechnikov carried the load up front while Hamilton contributed 40 points in 47 games. The duo of Mrazek and Reimer provided reliable goaltending and allowed the Hurricanes to play their game.

The team was rolling along nicely in the early season when the Calgary Flames paid a visit to PNC Arena. A first period goal by former Hurricane Elias Lindholm put the visitors ahead 1-0, a lead they carried into the third period. Carolina pressed, creating pressure in Calgary's zone, when Lucas Wallmark fed the puck to Andrei Svechnikov in the corner. The young wing carried it behind the net of David Rittich and stopped before lifting the puck on his stick blade and tucking into the corner above Rittich's right shoulder. Svechnikov had not only tied the game, he had made history as the first player to score a "lacrosse goal" in the NHL.

Just over three minutes later, he took a pass from Hamilton and wired a wrist shot past Rittich, putting the Hurricanes up 2-1. Carolina held on for the win, thanks to the heroics of the second year forward. Not content, Svechnikov would repeat the feat in a mid-December match with the Jets in Winnipeg. A little more than halfway in, the teams battled in a 2-2 tie when Svechnikov gathered a loose puck and skated behind the net. With ample room available, he flipped the puck onto his blade and beat Winnipeg's Connor Hellebuyck.

The Hurricanes went on to beat the Jets by a score of 6-3, with Sebastian Aho picking up the game-winning goal. Despite a few hiccups, they rolled into January with a record of 24-14-2, the fifth-best mark in the Eastern Conference. They weren't quite matching the pace of their previous season, but they were finding ways to win.

All the more impressive, they did it without their captain. Prior to the start of the season, Justin Williams announced he was taking some time away from the game. Then, on January 19, 2020, Williams made his first appearance of the season against the New York Islanders. The game would go deep into a shootout before the captain—Carolina's eight shooter—beat Thomas Greiss and secured the win.

While things were coming together nicely, Carolina was not immune to the injury bug. Haula—two years removed from a serious knee injury—suffered a setback and missed time. Jordan Martinook missed time after undergoing surgery to fix a core muscle injury. The biggest setback came when Hamilton broke the fibula in his left leg after falling awkwardly in a game against Columbus. The injury derailed an outstanding season for Hamilton and left a huge void in Carolina's power play.

Big news broke on February 15 when the league announced the Hurricanes would host the 2021 Stadium Series game at Carter-Finley Stadium. Started in 2014, the Stadium Series—regular season games played outdoors in football or baseball stadiums—became an incredibly popular event for the NHL, making this a big deal for the Hurricanes and hockey in North Carolina.

The Hurricanes carried on, gutting out wins despite their depleted lineup. They headed into the final week of February carrying a 34-22-4 record as they prepared to face the Maple Leafs in Toronto. By the end of the night, they would once again be at the center of the hockey world's attention. Reimer, six years a Leaf, got the start against his former team but didn't last long. Just over three minutes into the first period, Toronto forward Zach Hyman knocked Jaccob Slavin into his netminder, leading to Reimer exiting the game with a lower body injury.

Mrazek entered the game and played steady, allowing one goal on 16 shots. Eleven minutes into the second period, a Carolina pass was deflected down the ice and into their defensive zone; Mrazek came out to the top of the face-off circle to play the puck only to have Toronto's Kyle Clifford collide with him, dislodging his mask and sending the goalie hard to the ice. Tempers flared before Mrazek was escorted off; his night was done.

Naturally, having both of your goaltenders leave with injuries is less than ideal. That the Hurricanes were battling for playoff positioning only made it worse. Of course, this is a rare event, yet the NHL has a protocol in place. Each team in the league has an emergency backup goalie listed for their home arena. For Toronto, the man was David Ayres, the operations manager for the home arena of Toronto's AHL affiliate.

The 42-year-old entered the game, which the Hurricanes led 3-1, and promptly surrendered goals on the first two shots he faced. Carolina increased their defensive intensity and capitalized on their offensive opportunities, putting three more pucks past Toronto's Frederik Andersen. After the shaky start, Ayres stopped the next eight shots he faced and earned the win as the Hurricanes claimed a 6-3 victory. In doing so, he became the first emergency backup in NHL history to record a win. Beyond that, he became a mascot, celebrated by the team and the fans for his amazing story.

Even with the goodwill from Ayres' win, the team limped toward the trade deadline in need of help and Waddell provided. Defensemen Brady Skjei and Sami Vatanen joined the team while the GM packaged Haula to the Florida Panthers for center Vincent Trocheck. Skjei and Trocheck debuted soon after; Vatanen, injured at the time of the trade, experienced a setback in his recovery, leaving the timetable for him suiting up uncertain.

Then, two weeks after the deadline, the Coronavirus pandemic led the NHL to pause its season. The league stated that play would resume when it was "appropriate and prudent," but no one knew when that would be. Spring turned to summer when the league announced that the regular season would not be completed, but the Stanley Cup playoffs would begin on August 1, 2020. Because of health protocols, two sites would host all the games: Scotiabank Arena in Toronto for the East and Rogers Place in Edmonton for the West and the Stanley Cup Final.

Due to the circumstances, 24 teams would take part instead of the usual 16. The top four teams from each conference were seeded based on their points percentage at the time of the pause; the remaining 16 teams—including Carolina—would participate in best-of-five series to determine who would move on. The Hurricanes drew the New York Rangers, a team that swept them during the season.

To steal a well-worn phrase: once the playoffs start, the regular season doesn't matter. Carolina proved that, defeating New York in three straight, outscoring their opponent 11-4. The long layoff also afforded Vatanen time to heal and join his new team; the Finnish defender picked up three assists against the Rangers. Winning the series gave Carolina the right to face the Boston Bruins in the official first round and the added time allowed Hamilton to return to the lineup.

The Hurricanes entered the series eager to avenge being swept at the hands of the Bruins the year before; alas, it wasn't meant to be. Boston took the series in five games as Carolina struggled to find their game. Despite the short length of the series, the Hurricanes were not dominated, witnessed by the fact that four of the games were decided by one goal. Still, Carolina suffered an early elimination, a disappointing follow up to their previous run.

Prior to the 2020-21 season, the Hurricanes roster underwent a few minor tweaks: Edmundson, after one season in Raleigh, was traded to Montreal and speedy, two-way forward Jesper Fast came in as a free agent. The biggest change came when Justin Williams announced his retirement after 19 seasons. When returning to the team he won the 2006 Stanley Cup with, Williams stated he wanted the Hurricanes to be relevant again.

He certainly saw that come to fruition.

There were also changes to the league's alignment—albeit temporary ones—thanks to the ongoing pandemic, placing Carolina into a reformed Central Division:

2020-21 Central Division:
Carolina Hurricanes
Chicago Blackhawks
Columbus Blue Jackets
Dallas Stars
Detroit Red Wings
Florida Panthers
Nashville Predators
Tampa Bay Lightning

Another effect of the pandemic was the postponement of the Stadium Series game in Raleigh. The Hurricanes, wanting to ensure a safe environment, requested their game be moved to the 2022-23 season, a request the league granted. The league later announced that the Hurricanes would host the Washington Capitals at Carter-Finley on February 18, 2023.

Now, back to the season.

To compensate for the previous season's playoffs running until September 28, 2020, the league announced a 56-game schedule that would begin on January 13, 2021. The slate would feature divisional play exclusively, meaning the Hurricanes would see a lot of their seven division mates.

That was just fine by them.

Through their first ten games, Carolina racked up seven wins. Then, in a stretch from late February to mid-March, they pulled off an eight game win streak. More impressively, they did this without their number one goalie, as Petr Mrazek suffered a thumb injury in a late January match against the Dallas Stars. The damage required surgery, sidelining the Czech goalie until early April.

In his absence, the Hurricanes relied on Reimer as well as 26-year-old Alex Nedeljkovic. A second round pick in 2014, Nedeljkovic had cleared waivers in mid-January, just two weeks before Mrazek's injury. The Ohio native didn't miss a beat, tallying a 15-5-3 record in 23 appearances. Reimer also proved up to the task, going 15-5-2 in 22 games.

Goaltending proved not to be an area of worry. In fact, the offense and defense held up, leaving the Hurricanes with little to be concerned with. Injuries, however, stepped in to fill that void. The most notable loss was Teravainen, who missed a total of 35 games after contracting COVID-19 and suffering a concussion upon his initial return.

Gardiner, who had been providing solid, two-way play, was sidelined by recurring back issues, appearing in just 26 games. Brock McGinn had an upper body injury that sidelined him for 19 games; Vincent Trocheck missed nine games in his first full season with the Hurricanes.

Despite these setbacks, Carolina ended the regular season as division champions. They opened the playoffs against Nashville, a team they fared well against during the season. That trend continued through the first two games in the series with the Hurricanes winning both while outscoring the Predators 8-2. Nashville flipped the script in games three and four, a pair of tightly contested matches that both ended in double overtime, and both in favor of the Predators. Games five and six followed similar scripts, this time ending with Hurricanes' victories in overtime.

Nashville had pushed Carolina, and it's easy to see how, with a few bounces going the other way, the Hurricanes could have found themselves eliminated in the first round. Instead, they squared off with the defending champion Tampa Bay Lightning in round two, and the issues they struggled with against Nashville became insurmountable.

The more worrying trend came from the collapse of special teams. During the regular season, Carolina boasted the second-best power play in the league (25.61%) and third-best penalty kill (85.23%). While the power play took a dip again the Predators (21.05%), the penalty kill (88.46%) improved. In the series against Tampa Bay, both statistics took a nose-dive. Now, it's not surprising that a team with the Lightning's firepower would be dangerous on the man advantage, but their efficiency by series end was nearly 44%.

You're not misreading that; the Carolina penalty kill dropped to 56% in the series, a far cry from what they were capable of. The power play did not fare any better, with the Hurricanes netting just two goals in 14 opportunities, a conversion rate of 14.29%. Unsurprisingly, Tampa Bay eliminated Carolina in five games, dealing the Hurricanes another early playoff exit and leaving them with questions as to what they needed to do in order to get over the hump.

The summer of 2021 brought drastic changes throughout Carolina's lineup. Starting with the defense, Hamilton—a blueline fixture since his arrival in 2018—departed via free agency. Jake Bean, Carolina's first round pick from 2016, was dealt to Columbus. Waddell sent winger Warren Foegele to Edmonton for young defenseman Ethan Bear before turning his attention to the free agent market. The GM signed a handful of defenders in Ian Cole, Brendan Smith, Jalen Chatfield, and Tony DeAngelo, leaving Jaccob Slavin and Brett Pesce as the remaining cornerstones.

The forward corps also saw its fair share of turnover. Aside from Foegele, the team lost youngster Morgan Geekie to the Seattle Kraken during the expansion draft. Longtime Hurricane Brock McGinn—hero of the 2019 series against Washington—left for Pittsburgh. The most notable addition drew a bit of controversy when Waddell signed 21-year-old Montreal Canadiens' center Jesperi Kotkaniemi to a $6.1 million, one-year offer sheet. This came just two years after Montreal's unsuccessful attempt to lure away Sebastian Aho.

Almost immediately, speculation ran wild that Dundon orchestrated the Kotkaniemi signing as revenge for the failed attempt to poach Aho. There were plenty of definitive statements that the young Finn simply wasn't worth the price, which included first and third round draft picks. The rationale, however, is that the Hurricanes paid a premium in order to acquire a talented, young player who had yet to tap into his full potential. It was a risk that management was willing to take.

No area saw more retooling than goaltending. Alex Nedeljkovic—after playing a prominent role in preserving the Hurricanes' season—was traded to Detroit. Petr Mrazek, a key figure in ending Carolina's playoff drought, signed a three-year deal with Toronto. James Reimer, having provided two years of solid netminding, signed on with the San Jose Sharks. Just like that, the Hurricanes went from three solid goalies to none, paving the way for Waddell to rebuild the most important position on the team.

As the free agent market opened, Carolina's GM signed a pair of veterans to two-year deals. Antti Raanta was one half of a solid tandem in Arizona, never posting a save percentage below 90 in his four years there. During stints with the New York Rangers and Chicago Blackhawks, Raanta had played with current Hurricanes Teuvo Teravainen, Jesper Fast, and Brady Skjei, as well as playing with Jordan Martinook in Arizona.

The other half of Carolina's tandem would be a player that they drafted a decade before. Frederik Andersen, drafted by the Hurricanes in the third round of the 2010 draft, never signed with the team. At the time, Cam Ward was firmly entrenched as Carolina's starter and Andersen didn't see a path past him. Instead, he re-entered the draft in 2012. Anaheim selected him, and he spent three strong seasons there before moving to the Toronto Maple Leafs.

The Danish goaltender performed well, picking up 149 wins over five seasons, but often became the scapegoat for the team's lack of postseason success. During his final season in Toronto, a wonky knee cost Andersen nearly two months and opened the door for Jack Campbell to take over as the Leafs' number one.

LOOKING AHEAD

The Hurricanes, led by a young group of forwards, appear set for years of success. As of writing this, Carolina has just seven players over the age of 30, including both goaltenders. Of their key forwards (outside of captain Jordan Staal), Teravainen is the oldest at 27. Aho is 24; Svechnikov is just 21, as is the newly acquired Kotkaniemi. There are also a host of young players ready to step in, such as Seth Jarvis (19), Jack

Drury (22), Noel Gunler (20), Ryan Suzuki (20), and Jamieson Rees (21).

The defense, as it has been for years, is led by the duo of Slavin and Pesce, both 27. Brady Skjei (27), Ethan Bear (24), and Jalen Chatfield (25) should also play prominent roles. There's also a wealth of defensive prospects, including Scott Morrow (19), Alexander Nikishin (20), Aleksi Heimosalmi (18), and Ronan Seeley (19).

Carolina also possesses a nice stable of goaltending prospects, perhaps none more intriguing than Pyotr Kotchetkov (22). He's joined by Jack LaFontaine (24) and Eetu Makiniemi (22). Granted, we don't know how any of these young players will pan out, but the Hurricanes have a solid amount of touted prospects who have been performing well for their current teams. If a fair share can transfer that into NHL success, Carolina could be a top team in the league for years to come.

CHAPTER EIGHT

Team Leaders

CHARLOTTE REBELS
EHL

Games Played
Gerry Sullivan	63
Ken Murphy	63
Al O'Hearn	62
John Muckler	62
John Brophy	62
Russ Hann	61
Herb Schiller	58
Lloyd Buchanan	54
Eddie St. Louis	50
Willard Hass	40

Goals
Al O'Hearn	36
Gerry Sullivan	32
Herb Schiller	28
Lloyd Buchanan	18
Ken Murphy	17
C. Melanchuk	16
Willard Hass	15
Glen McKenney	12
John Muckler	11
Ralph DeLeo	10

Assists
Al O'Hearn	43
Ken Murphy	35
John Muckler	34
Gerry Sullivan	31
Lloyd Buchanan	30
Glen McKenney	28
Willard Hass	25
Herb Schiller	25
Russ Hann	21
Eddie St. Louis	18

Points
Al O'Hearn	79
Gerry Sullivan	63
Herb Schiller	53
Ken Murphy	52
Lloyd Buchanan	48
John Muckler	45
Willard Hass	40
Glen McKenney	40
C. Melanchuk	34
Russ Hann	31

Games Played (goaltender)
Les Binkley	59
Don O'Hearn	3
Woody Ryan	2

Wins*
Les Binkley	21

*goaltending records are incomplete

CHARLOTTE CLIPPERS
EHL

Games Played

Herve Lalonde	238
Jim McNulty	222
Ken Murphy	216
William Sinnett	202
John Muckler	187
Gerry Sullivan	181
John Brophy	181
Stan Warecki	175
Al O'Hearn	125
Yvan Houle	122

Goals

Jim McNulty	138
Doug Adam	109
Herve Lalonde	96
Al O'Hearn	79
Ken Murphy	77
Stan Warecki	76
Gerry Sullivan	70
Vern Jones	68
William Sinnett	64
Yvan Houle	46

Assists

Herve Lalonde	198
Jim McNulty	160
Stan Warecki	125
William Sinnett	122
Ken Murphy	121
Al O'Hearn	111
John Muckler	103
Gerry Sullivan	96
Doug Adam	82
Yvan Houle	80

Points

Jim McNulty	298
Herve Lalonde	294
Stan Warecki	201
Ken Murphy	198
Doug Adam	191
Al O'Hearn	190
William Sinnett	186
Gerry Sullivan	166
Vern Jones	132
John Muckler	128

Games Played (goaltender)

Les Binkley	128
Lynn Davis	66
Denis Brodeur	35
Norm Defelice	1

Wins*

Les Binkley	88
Lynn Davis	31

*goaltending records are incomplete

CHARLOTTE CHECKERS
EHL

Games Played

Maurice Savard	512
Jim McNulty	398
Bob Shupe	363
Ernie Dyda	336
Claude Ouimet	279
Barry Burnette	268
Ralph Winfield	259
Allie Sutherland	239
F. Golembrosky	236
Gaston Brassard	236

Goals

Maurice Savard	262
Jim McNulty	208
Claude Ouimet	159
F. Golembrosky	129
Allie Sutherland	127
Art Hart	109
Ernie Dyda	102
Gaston Brassard	95
Barry Simpson	86
Chuck Stuart	83

Assists

Maurice Savard	425
Jim McNulty	269
F. Golembrosky	188
Rick Foley	180
Claude Ouimet	170
Ernie Dyda	167
Barry Burnette	133
Michel Rouleau	131
Jack LeClair	123
Barry Simpson	119

Points

Maurice Savard	687
Jim McNulty	477
Claude Ouimet	329
F. Golembrosky	317
Ernie Dyda	269
Allie Sutherland	231
Art Hart	225
Rick Foley	224
Gaston Brassard	213
Michel Rouleau	213

Games Played (goaltender)

John Voss	122
G. Dessureault	118
Bob Whidden	115
Lynn Zimmerman	72

Wins*

-

*goaltending records are incomplete

CHARLOTTE CHECKERS
SHL

Games Played

Guy Burrowes	262
Barry Burnette	236
Gary Wood	225
Wayne Chrysler	204
Mike Keeler	190
Yvon Dupuis	189
John Morrison	180
Jack Wells	168
Bob Smulders	165
Neil Korzack	137

Goals

Yvon Dupuis	128
Wayne Chrysler	79
Neil Korzack	75
Guy Burrowes	70
Andre Deschamps	63
John Morrison	62
Steve Hull	59
Jack Wells	56
Bob Smulders	47
Mike Keeler	42

Assists

Guy Burrowes	153
Wayne Chrysler	145
Barry Burnette	129
Steve Hull	106
Gary Wood	104
Jack Wells	97
Yvon Dupuis	94
John Morrison	93
Mike Keeler	90
Bob Smulders	88

Points

Wayne Chrysler	224
Guy Burrowes	223
Yvon Dupuis	222
Steve Hull	165
Barry Burnette	165
John Morrison	155
Jack Wells	153
Neil Korzack	143
Bob Smulders	135
Mike Keeler	132

Games Played (goaltender)

Gaye Cooley	133
Dave Tataryn	39
Brian Cousineau	27
Don Muio	27
Bob Sauve	17
Danny Sullivan	11
Tim Regan	9
Bob Blanchet	7
Dan Brady	5
Jacques Lefebvre	2

Wins

Gaye Cooley	81
Dave Tataryn	20
Don Muio	16
Brian Cousineau	14
Bob Sauve	11
Danny Sullivan	9
Tim Regan	4
Bob Blanchet	1
Dan Brady	1

CHARLOTTE CHECKERS
ECHL

Games Played

Kurt Seher	593
Darryl Noren	365
Kenton Smith	330
Dusty Jamieson	298
Matt Robbins	256
Rory Rawlyk	205
David Brosseau	205
Kevin Hilton	202
Kenny Smith	188
J. F. Aube	186

Goals

Darryl Noren	174
Dusty Jamieson	139
Matt Robbins	113
David Brosseau	110
Sergei Berdnikov	85
J. F. Aube	84
Kurt Seher	73
Shawn Wheeler	68
Mike Bayrack	65
Kevin Hilton	62

Assists

Darryl Noren	229
Matt Robbins	227
Kurt Seher	203
Kevin Hilton	140
J. F. Aube	140
Kenton Smith	112
Dusty Jamieson	110
Eduard Pershin	90
Mike Bayrack	84
Nicholas Bilotto	76

Points

Darryl Noren	403
Matt Robbins	340
Kurt Seher	276
Dusty Jamieson	249
J. F. Aube	224
Kevin Hilton	202
David Brosseau	177
Sergei Berdnikov	161
Mike Bayrack	149
Kenton Smith	147

Games Played (goaltender)

Chris Holt	102
Scott Bailey	96
Scott Meyer	89
Nick Vitucci	84
Alex Westlund	78
Jeff Jakaitis	48
Jason Labarbera	48
Taras Lendzyk	48
Paxton Schafer	48
Ryan Munce	45

Wins

Nick Vitucci	52
Scott Meyer	49
Chris Holt	46
Alex Westlund	43
Scott Bailey	42
Jason Labarbera	27
Ryan Munce	26
Paxton Schafer	24
Jeff Jakaitis	23
Taras Lendzyk	18

CHARLOTTE CHECKERS
AHL

Games Played

Trevor Carrick	347
Zach Boychuk	337
Patrick Brown	334
Michal Jordan	301
Chris Terry	299
Rasmus Rissanen	294
Justin Shugg	271
Nicolas Blanchard	266
Brent Sutter	255
Dennis Robertson	239

Assists

Zach Boychuk	152
Chris Terry	150
Trevor Carrick	141
Andrew Poturalski	110
Justin Shugg	88
Brett Sutter	86
Patrick Brown	72
Michal Jordan	72
Bobby Sanguinetti	70
Andrew Miller	70

Games Played (goaltender)

John Muse	125
Alex Nedeljkovic	125
Mike Murphy	96
Drew MacIntyre	79
Justin Peters	71
Justin Pogge	48
Daniel Altshuller	43
Jeremy Smith	30
Michael Leighton	23
Dan Ellis	18

Goals

Zach Boychuk	123
Chris Terry	104
Andrew Poturalski	66
Justin Shugg	62
Zac Dalpe	62
Aleksi Saarela	61
Brett Sutter	56
Patrick Brown	53
Jerome Samson	53
Valentin Zykov	51

Points

Zach Boychuk	275
Chris Terry	254
Trevor Carrick	181
Andrew Poturalski	176
Justin Shugg	150
Brett Sutter	142
Zac Dalpe	131
Patrick Brown	125
Jerome Samson	109
Aleksi Saarela	107

Wins

Alex Nedeljkovic	73
John Muse	63
Mike Murphy	43
Justin Peters	36
Drew MacIntyre	31
Justin Pogge	22
Daniel Altshuller	17
Jeremy Smith	13
Michael Leighton	11
Tom McCollum	11

GREENSBORO GENERALS
EHL

Games Played

Don Carter	639
Ron Muir	632
Gary Sharp	481
Stu Roberts	438
Doug Carpenter	418
Don Burgess	363
Ron Quenville	341
Pat Kelly	337
Dom DiBerardino	290
Roger Wilson	281

Goals

Ron Muir	408
Gary Sharp	349
Don Carter	317
Stu Roberts	268
Dom DiBerardino	219
Don Burgess	190
Don Davidson	121
Les Lilley	114
Bob Sicinski	108
Bob Boucher	96

Assists

Don Carter	578
Ron Muir	422
Gary Sharp	403
Stu Roberts	279
Don Burgess	272
Pat Kelly	263
Dom DiBerardino	220
Don Davidson	213
Bob Sicinski	210
Ron Quenville	204

Points

Don Carter	895
Ron Muir	830
Gary Sharp	752
Stu Roberts	547
Don Burgess	462
Dom DiBerardino	439
Don Davidson	334
Bob Sicinski	318
Pat Kelly	302
Ron Quenville	271

Games Played (goaltender)

Jacques Monette	261
Ernie Miller	192
John Voss	129
Don Campbell	99
Bob Smith	69
Peter McDuffe	65
Steve Rexe	47
Mike Ralph	34
Don O'Hearn	6
Ludger Doucet	5

Wins*

-

*goaltending records are
incomplete

GREENSBORO GENERALS
SHL

Games Played

Wally Sprange	208
Howie Heggedal	153
Cam Colborne	151
Virgil Gates	133
Chris Leach	124
Ron Hindson	104
Alvin White	99
Allie Sutherland	89
Garry MacMillan	80
Jerry Zrymiak	77

Goals

Howie Heggedal	87
Wally Sprange	61
Cam Colborne	40
Stu Roberts	39
Allie Sutherland	38
Wayne Zuk	35
Rick Loe	34
Ken Gratton	31
Jacques Royer	28
Alvin White	24

Assists

Wally Sprange	164
Cam Colborne	90
Howie Heggedal	86
Kirk Bowman	55
Wayne Zuk	49
Mike Morton	47
Chris Leach	46
Jerry Zrymiak	44
Ron Hindson	42
Allie Sutherland	33

Points

Wally Sprange	225
Howie Heggedal	173
Cam Colborne	130
Wayne Zuk	84
Kirk Bowman	78
Allie Sutherland	71
Stu Roberts	67
Mike Morton	66
Rick Loe	60
Ron Hindson	60

Games Played (goaltender)

Steve Miskiewicz	48
Kevin Neville	39
Mike Ralph	37
Ernie Miller	33
Mike Corcoran	32
John Voss	27
Bob Perreault	16
Nick Sanza	13
Gordon Tumilson	11
Jacques Morin	8

Wins

Mike Ralph	15
Steve Miskiewicz	13
Ernie Miller	12
Mike Corcoran	10
Kevin Neville	8
Bob Perreault	7
John Voss	7
Gordon Tumilson	5
Nick Sanza	3
Bob Smith	2

GREENSBORO MONARCHS
ECHL

Games Played
Phil Berger	303
Darryl Noren	184
Boyd Sutton	171
Dean Zayonce	168
Scott White	156
Davis Payne	155
Chris Laganas	151
Chris Wolanin	136
Rob Bateman	123
Mike McCormick	110

Goals
Phil Berger	232
Darryl Noren	121
Boyd Sutton	77
Davis Payne	57
Shawn Wheeler	53
Chris Laganas	46
Scott White	41
Mike McCormick	40
Dan Bylsma	39
Dan Gravelle	38

Assists
Phil Berger	300
Darryl Noren	161
Scott White	126
Boyd Sutton	95
Doug Lawrence	86
Davis Payne	73
John Young	69
Dan Gravelle	67
Chris Valicevic	65
Chris Laganas	56

Points
Phil Berger	532
Darryl Noren	282
Boyd Sutton	172
Scott White	167
Davis Payne	130
Doug Lawrence	119
Shawn Wheeler	108
Dan Gravelle	105
John Young	104
Chris Laganas	102

Games Played (goaltender)
Nick Vitucci	111
Greg Menges	57
Tom Newman	49
Bill Horn	47
Patrick Labrecque	40
Peter Skudra	33
Wade Flaherty	30
Matt Merten	28
Rob Laurie	10
Ray Letourneau	10

Wins
Nick Vitucci	60
Bill Horn	29
Patrick Labrecque	23
Greg Menges	22
Tom Newman	22
Peter Skudra	13
Wade Flaherty	12
Matt Merten	12
Rob Laurie	4
Ray Letourneau	3

CAROLINA MONARCHS
AHL

Games Played

Chris Armstrong	144
Steve Washburn	138
Ashley Buckberger	136
Gilbert Dionne	127
Chad Cabana	114
Eric Montreuil	100
Trevor Doyle	95
Alain Nasreddine	89
Sean McCann	80
Ryan Johnson	79

Goals

Gilbert Dionne	84
Brad Smyth	68
Steve Washburn	52
Mike Casselman	34
Craig Fisher	33
Craig Ferguson	29
Todd Harkins	27
Brett Harkins	23
David Nemirovsky	22
Jason Podollan	21

Assists

Gilbert Dionne	105
Steve Washburn	94
Brett Harkins	71
Mike Casselman	68
Brad Smyth	58
Chris Armstrong	56
Craig Ferguson	41
Sean McCann	33
Craig Fisher	29
Todd Harkins	28

Points

Gilbert Dionne	189
Steve Washburn	146
Brad Smyth	126
Mike Casselman	102
Brett Harkins	94
Chris Armstrong	74
Craig Ferguson	70
Craig Fisher	62
Todd Harkins	55
Sean McCann	47

Games Played (goaltender)

Kevin Weekes	111
David Lemanowicz	33
Todd MacDonald	19
Jim Hrivnak	11
Mark Richards	1

Wins

Kevin Weekes	41
David Lemanowicz	11
Todd MacDonald	3
Jim Hrivnak	1

GREENSBORO GENERALS
ECHL

Games Played

Joel Irwin	209
David Whitworth	183
Sal Manganaro	182
Juraj Slovak	150
Geno Parrish	144
Mark Turner	142
Matt Turek	141
Matt Chandler	132
Chris Bell	117
Kurt Drummond	113

Goals

Sal Manganaro	79
Joel Irwin	62
Mark Turner	48
Sam Ftorek	44
Mike Bayrack	41
Matt Turek	40
David Whitworth	40
Chris Bell	32
Oleg Timchenko	32
Vlad Serov	31

Assists

David Whitworth	98
Joel Irwin	94
Geno Parrish	93
Mark Turner	93
Sal Manganaro	85
Kurt Drummond	70
Matt Turek	60
Chris Bell	53
Pete Gardiner	45
Mike Bayrack	44

Points

Sal Manganaro	164
Joel Irwin	156
Mark Turner	141
David Whitworth	138
Geno Parrish	109
Matt Turek	100
Kurt Drummond	87
Mike Bayrack	85
Chris Bell	85
Sam Ftorek	82

Games Played (goaltender)

Daniel Berthiaume	96
Jamie Hodson	44
Frederic Henry	39
Matt Eisler	36
Francis Larivee	31
Sergei Naumov	31
Trevor Prior	18
Bujar Amidovski	16
Eric Heffler	15
S. Centomo	10

Wins

Daniel Berthiaume	53
Jamie Hodson	26
Frederic Henry	14
Sergei Naumov	11
Matt Eisler	10
Francis Larivee	7
Bujar Amidovski	6
Trevor Prior	6
Eric Heffler	4
S. Centomo	3

WINSTON-SALEM POLAR TWINS
SHL

Games Played
Bill Morris	186
Ken Gassoff	172
John Campbell	164
Jamie Kennedy	141
Peter Williams	131
Brian Molvik	131
Ron Hindson	123
Tom Stachniak	111
Don Whelden	107
Bill Laing	102

Goals
Ken Gassoff	83
John Campbell	77
Bill Morris	65
Jamie Kennedy	59
Ron Hindson	40
Bernie Blanchette	39
Brian Carlin	36
Bill Laing	34
Greg Holst	33
Howie Colborne	33

Assists
Ken Gassoff	135
John Campbell	129
Bill Morris	96
Jamie Kennedy	73
Ron Hindson	70
Bill Laing	54
Tom Stachniak	49
Howie Colborne	48
Peter Williams	47
Ron Anderson	44

Points
Ken Gassoff	218
John Campbell	206
Bill Morris	161
Jamie Kennedy	132
Ron Hindson	110
Bill Laing	88
Howie Colborne	81
Brian Carlin	78
Bernie Blanchette	77
Ron Anderson	73

Games Played (goaltender)
Bob Champoux	92
Gary Doyle	75
Kevin Neville	35
Ken Brown	29
Danny Sullivan	27
Brian Cousineau	15
Pierre Mouton	4
Jim Watt	3
Jim Maertz	2

Wins
Bob Champoux	38
Gary Doyle	27
Danny Sullivan	12
Kevin Neville	11
Ken Brown	10
Brian Cousineau	3

CAROLINA THUNDERBIRDS
ACHL

Games Played

Randy Irving	277
Brian Carroll	265
Kim Elliot	235
Michel Lanouette	220
Bob Dore	196
Peter Dunkley	187
Bob Hagan	181
Dave Watson	168
John Torchetti	152
Joe Curran	144

Goals

Brian Carroll	156
Kim Elliot	133
Michel Lanouette	128
John Torchetti	116
Dave Watson	104
Joe Curran	89
Mike Brisebois	83
Peter Dunkley	71
Jay Fraser	57
Benoit Laporte	54

Assists

Brian Carroll	230
Kim Elliot	207
Randy Irving	196
Joe Curran	155
Michel Lanouette	155
Bob Hagan	142
Peter Dunkley	126
Dave Watson	122
Rory Cava	116
Doug McCarthy	116

Points

Brian Carroll	386
Kim Elliot	340
Michel Lanouette	283
Joe Curran	244
Randy Irving	242
John Torchetti	230
Dave Watson	226
Peter Dunkley	197
Bob Hagen	187
Doug McCarthy	169

Games Played (goaltender)

Dan Olson	84
Pierre Hamel	74
Ray LeBlanc	42
Yves Dechene	29
Paul Skidmore	29
Tom Allen	26
Mark Liska	23
Bruce Gillies	20
Jim Warden	19
Grant McNichol	12

Wins

Pierre Hamel	53
Dan Olson	34*
Ray LeBlanc	33
Yves Dechene	24
Mark Liska	16
Paul Skidmore	14
Jim Warden	9*

*goaltending records are incomplete

CAROLINA THUNDERBIRDS
AAHL

Games Played
John Torchetti	49
Sean Mangan	45
Steve Plaskon	44
Frank Lattuca	44
Dean Dixon	42
Brad Hammett	41
Todd Delveaux	39
Scott Allen	38
Tad Merritt	32
Michel Lanouette	28

Goals
John Torchetti	63
Steve Plaskon	41
Dean Dixon	33
Scott Allen	31
Michel Lanouette	28
Rick Brebant	25
Brad Hammett	16
Mike Kuzmich	14
Paul Reifenberger	11
Todd Delveaux	11

Assists
John Torchetti	71
Steve Plaskon	65
Brad Hammett	52
Frank Lattuca	41
Dean Dixon	33
Michel Lanouette	28
Scott Allen	28
Tad Merritt	27
Sean Mangan	27
Rick Brebant	24

Points
John Torchetti	134
Steve Plaskon	106
Brad Hammett	68
Dean Dixon	66
Scott Allen	59
Michel Lanouette	56
Rick Brebant	49
Frank Lattuca	46
Mike Kuzmich	36
Sean Mangan	36

Games Played (goaltender)
Mike Schwalb	26
Bruce Gillies	17
Pete Richards	9
Toby O'Brien	2
Dan Olson	2

Wins*
N/A   -

*goaltending records are incomplete

CAROLINA THUNDERBIRDS
ECHL

Games Played

Bob Wensley	60
Frank Lattuca	51
Blair McReynolds	48
Bill Huard	40
Scott Allen	40
Brian Hannon	39
Jay Fraser	37
E. J. Sauer	34
Jeff Greene	33
John Torchetti	30

Goals

Brian Hannon	30
Bill Huard	27
E. J. Sauer	21
Bob Wensley	21
John Devereaux	18
Blair McReynolds	18
John Torchetti	16
Jay Fraser	16
Scott Allen	16
John Dzikowski	10

Assists

Blair McReynolds	39
Frank Lattuca	38
Brian Hannon	37
Bob Wensley	32
John Devereaux	31
Jay Fraser	28
John Torchetti	26
Scott Allen	21
Bill Huard	21
Steve Plaskon	19

Points

Brian Hannon	67
Blair McReynolds	57
Bob Wensley	53
John Devereaux	49
Bill Huard	48
Frank Lattuca	46
Jay Fraser	44
John Torchetti	42
E. J. Sauer	38
Scott Allen	37

Games Played (goaltender)

Nick Vitucci	22
Mike Schwalb	17
Gary Willett	17
Dan Gatenby	6
Shaun O'Sullivan	4
Kenton Rein	4
Toby O'Brien	3

Wins*

Nick Vitucci	11

*goaltending records are incomplete

WINSTON-SALEM THUNDERBIRDS
ECHL

Games Played

Brent Fleetwood	117
John Devereaux	117
Troy Vollhoffer	110
John Torchetti	94
Bob Wensley	91
Joe Ferras	69
Jamie Russell	64
Doug Greschuk	64
Devin Edgerton	64
Len Soccio	60

Goals

Troy Vollhoffer	63
Joe Ferras	62
Trent Kaese	56
Brent Fleetwood	55
Len Soccio	51
John Devereaux	43
John Torchetti	42
Devin Edgerton	40
Derek DeCosty	30
Trevor Sim	25

Assists

John Devereaux	86
Joe Ferras	86
Troy Vollhoffer	82
Brent Fleetwood	64
Len Soccio	62
Keith Gretzky	51
Trent Kaese	51
Craig Endean	46
John Torchetti	43
Dan Woodley	42

Points

Joe Ferras	148
Troy Vollhoffer	145
John Devereaux	129
Brent Fleetwood	119
Len Soccio	113
Trent Kaese	107
John Torchetti	85
Devin Edgerton	82
Craig Endean	71
Keith Gretzky	66

Games Played (goaltender)

Kenton Rein	57
Mike Millham	38
Frederic Chabot	25
Paul Cohen	18
Alain Morissette	18
John Fletcher	12
Nick Vitucci	6
Tom Dennis	5
George Maneluk	3
Jocelyn Provost	3

Wins

Kenton Rein	25
Mike Millham	17
Frederic Chabot	15
Paul Cohen	12
Alain Morissette	10
Nick Vitucci	4
Tom Dennis	3
George Maneluk	2
Jocelyn Provost	1
Gus Morschauser	1

WINSTON-SALEM MAMMOTHS
SHL

Games Played	
Bruno Villeneuve	60
Hayden O'Rear	60
Alain Cote	60
Tom Moulton	59
Alexei Deev	59
Travis Hulse	58
Gord Kalverda	56
Mike DeGurse	56
Kirk Llano	55
Yvan Corbin	47

Goals	
Yvan Corbin	52
Alexei Deev	37
Bruno Villeneuve	23
Jamie Allan	20
John Devereaux	19
Alain Cote	19
Mike DeGurse	18
Mark McFarlane	14
Gord Kalverda	12
Rob Mencunas	11

Assists	
Alexei Deev	51
Yvan Corbin	43
Jamie Allan	35
Hayden O'Rear	34
Bruno Villeneuve	33
John Devereaux	32
Travis Hulse	31
Kirk Llano	26
Tom Moulton	26
Alain Cote	25

Points	
Yvan Corbin	95
Alexei Deev	88
Bruno Villeneuve	56
Jamie Allan	55
John Devereaux	51
Alain Cote	44
Hayden O'Rear	40
Mike DeGurse	38
Travis Hulse	34
Tom Moulton	31

Games Played (goaltender)	
Wayne Marion	49
George Bosak	21

Wins	
Wayne Marion	25
George Bosak	5

WINSTON-SALEM ICEHAWKS
UHL

Games Played

Larry Empey	145
Shawn Yakimishyn	120
Dmitri Suur	101
Trent Schachle	74
Steve Richards	74
Alexei Deev	74
Darren Schwartz	73
Jeffrey Azar	71
Jarrett Whidden	70
Dean Zayonce	69

Assists

Dmitri Suur	54
Alexei Deev	49
Shawn Yakimishyn	46
Jeffrey Azar	45
Sergei Petrov	39
Trent Schachle	35
Keith Osborne	35
Darren Schwartz	35
Jarrett Whidden	34
Trevor Senn	28

Games Played (goaltender)

Brian Kreft	33
Mark Richards	33
Marc Delorme	27
Bill Horn	24
Martin Bradette	17
Ryan Caley	14
Darren Thomas	12
Jason White	3

Goals

Darren Schwartz	42
Jeffrey Azar	38
Shawn Yakimishyn	36
Alexei Deev	35
Sergei Petrov	30
Keith Osborne	26
Jarrett Whidden	24
Dmitri Suur	17
Paul Vincent	16
Trent Schachle	14

Points

Alexei Deev	84
Jeffrey Azar	83
Shawn Yakimishyn	82
Darren Schwartz	77
Dmitri Suur	71
Sergei Petrov	69
Keith Osborne	61
Jarrett Whidden	58
Trent Schachle	49
Steve Richards	40

Wins

Mark Richards	16
Marc Delorme	12
Bill Horn	12
Brian Kreft	11
Martin Bradette	5
Ryan Caley	4
Darren Thomas	3
Jason White	1

WINSTON-SALEM PARROTS
ACHL

Games Played

John Gurskis	57
Andrew Dickson	57
Sam Miller	56
Ken Fels	54
Rob Schweyer	51
Colin Young	49
Jon Austin	49
Matt Holmes	48
Doug Merrell	43
Tom McMonagle	43

Goals

Matt Holmes	22
Janis Tomans	16
Roger Holeczy	14
Tom McMonagle	14
Doug Merrell	13
John Gurskis	13
Chris Cerrella	11
Jon Austin	11
Rob Schweyer	9
Rob Frost	8

Assists

John Gurskis	40
Rob Schweyer	29
Roger Holeczy	27
Jon Austin	25
Andrew Dickson	23
Matt Holmes	22
Tom McMonagle	16
Doug Merrell	14
Janis Tomans	13
Colin Young	11

Points

John Gurskis	53
Matt Holmes	44
Roger Holeczy	41
Rob Schweyer	38
Jon Austin	36
Andrew Dickson	31
Tom McMonagle	30
Janis Tomans	29
Doug Merrell	27
Chris Cerrella	20

Games Played (goaltender)

Dan McIntyre	26
Dean Weasler	14
Andy Kollar	12
Michal Lanicek	9
Bill Horn	2
Ray Fraser	1

Wins

Dan McIntyre	16
Dean Weasler	8
Andy Kollar	2
Michal Lanicek	2

WINSTON-SALEM T-BIRDS
SEHL

Games Played
Chris Seifert	55
Marcus Willy	54
Matt Lefaive	50
Jim Lundwall	47
Jason Sangiuliano	44
B. J. Heckendorn	43
Kevin Carr	36
Derek Kern	35
Jason Silverthorn	33
David Vychodil	31

Goals
Chris Seifert	26
Frantisek Bakrlik	18
Bryan Lachapelle	17
Jason Sangiuliano	14
Marcus Willy	14
Jason Silverthorn	13
Matt Lefaive	12
Peter Cermak	10
Derek Kern	8
Dan Howard	7

Assists
Chris Seifert	32
Jason Sangiuliano	20
Derek Kern	18
Matt Lefaive	18
Jason Silverthorn	18
Marcus Willy	18
B. J. Heckendorn	14
Peter Cermak	14
David Vychodil	13
Jim Lubinski	13

Points
Chris Seifert	58
Jason Sangiuliano	34
Marcus Willy	32
Jason Silverthorn	31
Frantisek Bakrlik	30
Matt Lefaive	30
Bryan Lachapelle	28
Derek Kern	26
Peter Cermak	24
Jim Lubinski	20

Games Played (goaltender)
Cam McCormick	36
Terry Craven	12
Martin Kresac	12
Adam Barbour	4

Wins
Cam McCormick	10
Terry Craven	4
Martin Kresac	3
Adam Barbour	1

WINSTON-SALEM POLAR TWINS
SPHL

Games Played

Shaun Aebig	56
Rhett Dudley	54
Steve Lajoie	53
T. Karasiewicz	52
Marcus Willy	49
Graham Dearle	47
R. Gustafsson	42
Mike Walling	34
Chester Gallant	34
Bill Cass	30

Goals

Shaun Aebig	27
T. Karasiewicz	17
Brett Cross	14
Steve Lajoie	14
Chester Gallant	13
Graham Dearle	12
Rhett Dudley	9
Justin Kot	8
Geoff Rollins	8
Troy Ilijow	8

Assists

T. Karasiewicz	43
Shaun Aebig	34
Marcus Willy	31
Steve Lajoie	29
Rhett Dudley	18
Geoff Rollins	15
Trevor Jobe	13
R. Gustafsson	11
Troy Ilijow	10
Graham Dearle	10

Points

Shaun Aebig	61
T. Karasiewicz	60
Steve Lajoie	43
Marcus Willy	34
Rhett Dudley	27
Brett Cross	24
Geoff Rollins	23
Graham Dearle	22
Chester Gallant	21
Trevor Jobe	20

Games Played (goaltender)

Jomar Cruz	28
Rick Nichol	17
Nathan Grobins	13
Scott Gouthro	5
Randy Hevey	1
Cam McCormick	1

Wins

Jomar Cruz	8
Nathan Grobins	3
Rick Nichol	2
Scott Gouthro	1

TWIN CITY CYCLONES
SPHL

Games Played

Taylor Hustead	98
Brady Heintz	86
Allan Sirois	85
Ryan Bartle	85
Paul Falco	81
Steve Obelnicki	74
Matt Puntureri	66
Josh Piro	65
Daryl Moore	62
Mike Richard	60

Assists

Taylor Hustead	59
Don Melnyk	51
Daryl Moore	51
Mike Richard	43
Allan Sirois	42
Jason Cassells	40
John Gurskis	35
Paul Falco	28
Shane Wagner	24
C. Swartzentruber	23

Games Played (goaltender)

Kevin Druce	62
Terry Dunbar	32
Adam Geragosian	18
Nick Pannoni	10
S. Conschafter	4
Peter Vetri	2

Goals

Taylor Hustead	49
Allan Sirois	43
Daryl Moore	36
Mike Richard	29
Don Melnyk	26
Matt Puntureri	26
Ben Manny	25
Jason Cassells	22
Steve Obelnicki	18
John Gurskis	17

Points

Taylor Hustead	108
Daryl Moore	87
Allan Sirois	85
Don Melnyk	77
Mike Richard	72
Jason Cassells	62
John Gurskis	52
Matt Puntureri	48
Paul Falco	40
Ben Manny	39

Wins

Kevin Druce	25
Terry Dunbar	10
Adam Geragosian	7
Nick Pannoni	6

CAROLINA THUNDERBIRDS
FHL

Games Played

Jiri Pestuka	157
Joe Cangelosi	143
Jan Salak	137
Michael Bunn	130
Stanislav Vlasov	125
Petr Panacek	124
Dominik Fejt	109
Josh Pietrantonio	100
Viktor Grebennikov	99
Seth Gustin	97

Goals

Jan Salak	69
Michael Bunn	67
Petr Panacek	48
Josh Pietrantonio	46
Kalib Ford	43
Jon Buttitta	40
Jiri Pestuka	36
Chase Fallis	33
Jiri Pargac	30
Joe Cangelosi	29

Assists

Jan Salak	114
Petr Panacek	100
Josh Pietrantonio	93
Michael Bunn	78
Jiri Pestuka	70
Jon Buttitta	65
Joe Cangelosi	64
Jiri Pargac	59
Stanislav Vlasov	52
Chase Fallis	48

Points

Jan Salak	183
Petr Panacek	148
Michael Bunn	145
Josh Pietrantonio	139
Jiri Pestuka	106
Jon Buttitta	105
Joe Cangelosi	93
Jiri Pargac	89
Kalib Ford	84
Chase Fallis	81

Games Played (goaltender)

Chris Paulin	77
Christian Pavlas	61
Nick Modica	37
Kelly Curl	29
F. McClendon	29
Henry Dill	27
Patrik Polivka	23
Jacob Mullen	16
Brandon Rozzi	16
Cary Byron	12

Wins

Christian Pavlas	38
Chris Paulin	31
Henry Dill	18
F. McClendon	14
Patrik Polivka	11
Kelly Curl	10
Nick Modica	9
Jacob Mullen	9
Cary Byron	5
Brandon Rozzi	4

PINEBRIDGE BUCKS
ACHL

Games Played
Frank Perkins	90
Kelly Rissling	75
Dave Burke	70
Scott Robins	64
Steve Atwell	64
Peter Dunkley	63
Tom Madson	62
Ken Latta	60
Larry Mollard	60
Rob Clavette	59

Goals
Rob Clavette	105
Scott Robins	53
Ken Latta	43
Todd Bjorkstrand	41
Dave Burke	34
Peter Dunkley	33
Kim Collins	32
Dan Potter	27
Mike Tompkins	26
Kelly Rissling	25

Assists
Rob Clavette	140
Frank Perkins	82
Scott Robins	57
Dave Burke	55
Tom Madson	51
Peter Dunkley	49
Kelly Rissling	48
Dave Dziedzic	46
Ken Latta	43
Todd Bjorkstrand	42

Points
Rob Clavette	245
Scott Robins	110
Frank Perkins	107
Dave Burke	89
Ken Latta	86
Todd Bjorkstrand	83
Peter Dunkley	82
Kelly Rissling	73
Dave Dziedzic	68
Kim Collins	67

Games Played (goaltender)
Steve Heittola	81
Ray LeBlanc	40
Dan Burrows	20
Don Sylvestri	6
Mark Walton	3
Todd Pearson	2

Wins
Steve Heittola	30
Ray LeBlanc	18
Dan Burrows	7
Don Sylvestri	2

ASHEVILLE SMOKE
UHL

Games Played
Shawn Ulrich	213
Bobby Rapoza	145
Lindsay Vallis	135
Jon Pirrong	135
Kris Schultz	130
Tom Wilson	122
Bruce Watson	121
Cory Peterson	117
Brent Gretzky	106
J. C. Ruid	104

Goals
Shawn Ulrich	102
Brent Gretzky	64
J. C. Ruid	59
Jeff Petruic	57
Lindsay Vallis	51
Frank DeFrenza	48
Dominic Maltais	40
J-F Dufour	40
Peter Cermak	31
Bogdan Rudenko	28

Assists
Shawn Ulrich	136
Brent Gretzky	134
Lindsay Vallis	125
J. C. Ruid	72
J-F Dufour	65
Brett Colborne	62
Dominic Maltais	61
Bobby Rapoza	59
Jeff Petruic	57
Derek Crimin	56

Points
Shawn Ulrich	238
Brent Gretzky	198
Lindsay Vallis	176
J. C. Ruid	131
Jeff Petruic	114
J-F Dufour	105
Dominic Maltais	101
Derek Crimin	84
Frank DeFrenza	83
Bobby Rapoza	77

Games Played (goaltender)
Brent Belecki	56
Danny Laviolette	50
Blaine Russell	49
Dan McIntyre	40
Lee Schill	34
Dan Brenzavich	23
Geoff Derouin	18
Mark Scally	15
Alex Fomitchev	14
Sergei Tkachenko	12

Wins
Brent Belecki	34
Danny Laviolette	25
Blaine Russell	21
Dan McIntyre	17
Lee Schill	13
Geoff Derouin	10
Dan Brenzavich	9
Alex Fomitchev	9
Sergei Tkachenko	6
Mark Scally	5

ASHEVILLE ACES
SPHL

Games Played

Martin Viazanica	56
Jan Kentos	54
Dan Pszenyczny	51
Brett Roat	49
Joel Petkoff	48
Jarno Mensonen	44
Peter Bournazakis	43
N. Kinugasa	40
Peter Cermak	37
Dan Beland	32

Assists

Peter Bournazakis	34
Dan Pszenyczny	26
Brett Roat	25
Joel Petkoff	25
Jarno Mensonen	24
Martin Viazanica	21
Dan Beland	16
Peter Cermak	16
Chad Brandimore	15
Janis Tomans	10

Games Played (goaltender)

Mark Scally	39
Ryan Person	18
Nick Niedert	3
Jorge Alves	2

Goals

Peter Bournazakis	22
Joel Petkoff	22
Brett Roat	20
Janis Tomans	14
Peter Cermak	12
Chris Ferguson	10
Martin Viazanica	10
Eldon Cheechoo	7
Chad Brandimore	7
Dan Beland	7

Points

Peter Bournazakis	56
Joel Petkoff	47
Brett Roat	45
Dan Pszenyczny	35
Martin Viazanica	31
Jarno Mensonen	31
Peter Cermak	28
Janis Tomans	24
Dan Beland	23
Chad Brandimore	22

Wins

Mark Scally	14
Ryan Person	5

RALEIGH ICECAPS
ECHL

Games Played

Lyle Wildgoose	306
Jim Powers	203
Derek Linnell	189
Darren Colbourne	157
Spencer Meany	155
Rick Barkovich	136
Alan Leggett	125
Todd Person	114
Steve Potvin	111
Chic Pojar	109

Goals

Lyle Wildgoose	150
Darren Colbourne	110
Jim Powers	90
Rick Barkovich	79
Kevin Riehl	44
Kirby Lindal	42
Steve Potvin	42
Derek Linnell	41
Kory Karlander	40
Bruno Villeneuve	35

Assists

Lyle Wildgoose	210
Jim Powers	138
Rick Barkovich	102
Darren Colbourne	88
Kris Miller	74
Steve Potvin	70
Kory Karlander	68
Jeff Reid	65
Alan Leggett	64
Kevin Riehl	60

Points

Lyle Wildgoose	360
Jim Powers	228
Darren Colbourne	198
Rick Barkovich	181
Steve Potvin	112
Kory Karlander	108
Kevin Riehl	104
Kris Miller	97
Derek Linnell	96
Kirby Lindal	90

Games Played (goaltender)

Brad Mullahy	80
Stan Reddick	48
Chad Erickson	43
P. Charbonneau	40
Joaquin Gage	39
Wayne Cowley	38
Frederic Henry	34
Matt DelGuidice	32
Bill Horn	29
Jim Mill	29

Wins

Brad Mullahy	27
Stan Reddick	24
Chad Erickson	20
Joaquin Gage	19
P. Charbonneau	18
Matt DelGuidice	18
Wayne Cowley	16
Jim Mill	16
Frederic Henry	13
Bill Horn	7

FAYETTEVILLE FORCE
CHL

Games Played
Rod MacCormick	204
Colin Muldoon	184
Alex Chunchukov	171
Jasen Rintala	165
Justin Tomberlin	138
Chris Ford	136
Ryan Schmidt	132
Darren McLean	126
Steven Toll	109
Ronalds Ozolinsh	101

Goals
Justin Tomberlin	72
Alex Chunchukov	68
Rod MacCormick	57
Darryl Noren	48
Chris Ford	46
Steven Toll	42
Jeffrey Azar	39
Chad Remackel	36
S. Sangermano	35
Jamie Steer	32

Assists
Alex Chunchukov	131
Rod MacCormick	121
Brett Colborne	71
Chad Remackel	67
Justin Tomberlin	65
Steven Toll	64
Chris Ford	62
Jamie Steer	51
Aaron Boh	43
David Hoogsteen	43

Points
Alex Chunchukov	199
Rod MacCormick	178
Justin Tomberlin	137
Chris Ford	108
Steven Toll	106
Chad Remackel	103
Brett Colborne	102
Darryl Noren	84
Jamie Steer	83
S. Sangermano	76

Games Played (goaltender)
Ken Shepard	92
Nathan Grobins	42
Ian Olsen	35
Troy Seibel	27
Paul Taylor	25
Trent Mann	22
Dan Dennis	16
Mark Bernard	15
Chris Bernard	13
Colum Cavilla	13

Wins
Ken Shepard	49
Nathan Grobins	24
Ian Olsen	14
Paul Taylor	12
Dan Dennis	8
Trent Mann	7
Chris Bernard	6
Mark Bernard	6
Troy Seibel	5
Colum Cavilla	4

CAPE FEAR FIRE ANTZ
ACHL

Games Played

Sean Fitzgerald	60
Peter Cermak	60
Aaron Shrieves	54
Matt Kohansky	53
Ryan Kiley	53
Martin Belanger	51
Mike Fournier	48
Steve Burgess	47
Marc Genest	46
Ryan Olson	40

Goals

Ryan Kiley	26
Matt Kohansky	23
Aaron Shrieves	23
Peter Cermak	21
Bruce Watson	20
Marc Genest	15
Ryan Olson	12
Chris Migliore	8
Dwight Wolfe	5
Mike Fournier	4

Assists

Peter Cermak	53
Matt Kohansky	38
Marc Genest	23
Bruce Watson	21
Martin Belanger	18
Ryan Kiley	17
Sean Fitzgerald	15
Mike Fournier	12
Dwight Wolfe	12
Aaron Shrieves	12

Points

Peter Cermak	74
Matt Kohansky	61
Ryan Kiley	43
Bruce Watson	41
Marc Genest	38
Aaron Shrieves	35
Ryan Olson	22
Martin Belanger	21
Sean Fitzgerald	19
Dwight Wolfe	17

Games Played (goaltender)

Geoff Derouin	37
Ken Shepard	30
Paul Schonfelder	3

Wins

Ken Shepard	13
Geoff Derouin	8

CAPE FEAR FIRE ANTZ
SEHL

Games Played
Marc Milburn	56
Matt Shannon	50
Matt Kohansky	50
Dave Leger	49
David Bagley	47
Mike Maurice	44
Aaron Shrieves	43
Chris Migliore	41
Scott Young	36
Tim Rink	33

Goals
David Bagley	28
Matt Kohansky	25
Chris Migliore	20
Ryan Kiley	19
Mike Maurice	16
Scott Young	11
Marc Milburn	10
Mike Bournazakis	10
Aaron Shrieves	9
Peter Cermak	9

Assists
Matt Kohansky	36
David Bagley	32
Scott Young	27
Mike Bournazakis	21
Chris Migliore	19
R. J. Roy	17
Mike Maurice	17
Chris Bodnar	13
Tim Rink	12
Rob Vessio	12

Points
Matt Kohansky	61
David Bagley	60
Chris Migliore	39
Scott Young	38
Mike Maurice	33
Mike Bournazakis	31
Ryan Kiley	28
Chris Bodnar	22
Marc Milburn	20
Peter Cermak	19

Games Played (goaltender)
Kevin Fines	22
Trevor Prior	16
Glenn Ridler	15
Geoff Derouin	6
Kevin Block	1

Wins
Kevin Fines	11
Glenn Ridler	8
Trevor Prior	5
Geoff Derouin	1

FAYETTEVILLE FIREANTZ
SPHL

Games Played

Bobby Reed	275
Rob Sich	245
Chris Leveille	222
Kyle McNeil	219
Derek Elliott	203
Josh McQuade	184
Sean Cryer	174
Craig Geerlinks	172
Corey Hessler	168
John Clewlow	155

Goals

Rob Sich	198
Josh McQuade	98
Chris Leveille	92
Bobby Reed	63
B. J. Stephens	60
Tim Velemirovich	53
George Nistas	52
John Clewlow	49
Josh Welter	48
Derek Elliott	47

Assists

Chris Leveille	173
Rob Sich	164
Josh McQuade	116
Bobby Reed	111
Tim Velemirovich	107
Mike Clarke	90
Derek Elliott	89
Josh Welter	84
Kory Baker	79
Corey Hessler	77

Points

Rob Sich	362
Chris Leveille	265
Josh McQuade	214
Bobby Reed	174
Tim Velemirovich	160
B. J. Stephens	136
Derek Elliott	136
Josh Welter	132
Jesse Biduke	113
Kory Baker	109

Games Played (goaltender)

Chad Collins	174
Sean Bonar	66
Guy St. Vincent	55
Glenn Ridler	43
Parker Van Buskirk	43
Marco Emond	42
Mike Brown	40
Kyle Knechtel	38
Peter Skoggard	37
Kevin Murdock	33

Wins

Chad Collins	94
Sean Bonar	43
Guy St. Vincent	30
Marco Emond	25
Glenn Ridler	23
Parker Van Buskirk	21
Kyle Knechtel	15
Kevin Murdock	15
Peter Skoggard	15
Mike Brown	14

FAYETTEVILLE MARKSMEN
SPHL

Games Played
Taylor McCloy	130
Travis Jeke	121
Jake Hauswirth	107
Max Cook	106
Tim Kielich	99
Donald Olivieri	90
Brian Bowen	81
Shane Bednard	74
Jarret Kup	72
Nolan Sheeran	64

Goals
Brian Bowen	47
Jake Hauswirth	47
Taylor McCloy	46
Max Cook	30
Darren McCormick	23
Taylor Best	22
Donald Olivieri	22
Drake Glover	21
Shane Bednard	18
Tim Kielich	18

Assists
Max Cook	78
Travis Jeke	56
Taylor McCloy	56
Shane Bednard	55
Jake Hauswirth	55
Brian Bowen	51
Donald Olivieri	45
Nolan Sheeran	31
Taylor Best	29
Tim Kielich	28

Points
Max Cook	108
Jake Hauswirth	102
Taylor McCloy	102
Brian Bowen	98
Shane Bednard	73
Travis Jeke	68
Donald Olivieri	67
Taylor Best	51
Tim Kielich	46
Drake Glover	45

Games Played (goaltender)
Dillon Kelley	36
Blake Wojtala	28
Patrick Spano	26
Jason Pawloski	24
Brent Moran	21
Nathan Perry	19
Peter Di Salvo	17
Stefano Durante	10
Danny Tirone	9
Alex Murray	8

Wins
Jason Pawloski	18
Blake Wojtala	18
Brent Moran	17
Dillon Kelley	13
Nathan Perry	9
Danny Tirone	7
Peter Di Salvo	5
Stefano Durante	5
Patrick Spano	3
Alex Murray	2

CAROLINA HURRICANES
NHL

Games Played

Eric Staal	909
Glen Wesley	729
Rod Brind'Amour	694
Jordan Staal	657
Jeff Skinner	579
Justin Faulk	559
Erik Cole	557
Tim Gleason	546
Jeff O'Neill	536
Niclas Wallin	517

Goals

Eric Staal	322
Jeff Skinner	204
Sebastian Aho	180
Jeff O'Neill	176
Rod Brind'Amour	174
Erik Cole	168
Jordan Staal	137
Justin Williams	128
Sami Kapanen	127
Ray Whitney	119

Assists

Eric Staal	453
Rod Brind'Amour	299
Ron Francis	236
Jordan Staal	224
Teuvo Teravainen	222
Sebastian Aho	216
Ray Whitney	215
Erik Cole	195
Justin Williams	188
Sami Kapanen	187

Points

Eric Staal	775
Rod Brind'Amour	473
Sebastian Aho	396
Jeff Skinner	379
Erik Cole	363
Jordan Staal	361
Jeff O'Neill	359
Ron Francis	354
Ray Whitney	334
Teuvo Teravainen	320

Games Played (goaltender)

Cam Ward	668
Arturs Irbe	309
Kevin Weekes	119
Petr Mrazek	92
Trevor Kidd	72
Anton Khudobin	70
Justin Peters	68
Martin Gerber	60
Eddie Lack	54
Frederik Andersen	52

Wins

Cam Ward	318
Arturs Irbe	130
Petr Mrazek	50
Kevin Weekes	39
Martin Gerber	38
Frederik Andersen	35
James Reimer	29
Trevor Kidd	28
Anton Khudobin	27
Justin Peters	22

CHAMPIONSHIPS

Season	Team	League
1956-57	Charlotte Clippers	EHL
1962-63	Greensboro Generals	EHL
1970-71	Charlotte Checkers	EHL
1971-72	Charlotte Checkers	EHL
1975-76	Charlotte Checkers	SHL
1982-83	Carolina Thunderbirds	ACHL
1984-85	Carolina Thunderbirds	ACHL
1985-86	Carolina Thunderbirds	ACHL
1988-89	Carolina Thunderbirds	ECHL
1989-90	Greensboro Monarchs	ECHL
1995-96	Charlotte Checkers	ECHL
2005-06	Carolina Hurricanes	NHL
2006-07	Fayetteville FireAntz	SPHL
2018-19	Charlotte Checkers	AHL
2018-19	Carolina Thunderbirds	FHL

CHAMPIONSHIPS BY CITY

Charlotte	6
Winston-Salem	5
Greensboro	2
Raleigh	1
Fayetteville	1

NOTES

1. QUEEN CITY ORIGINS

1. Atwater, Edward C; (1956, January 24). Action Now Awaits Only League O.K. *The Baltimore Sun,* p19
2. Pierce, Dick; (1958, March 23). Two Local Shareholders To Buy All Clipper Stock. *The Charlotte Observer,* p29
3. Green, Ronald; (1960, February 5). Rock Denies He's Selling Clippers. *The Charlotte Observer,* p16
4. Quincy, Bob; (1958, April 12). Three Incidents Hurt Clipper Playoffs; Club Traveled 26,000 Miles During Year. *The Charlotte Observer,* p7
5. Quincy, Bob; (1958, April 12). Three incidents Hurt Clipper Playoffs; Club Traveled 26,000 Miles During Year. *The Charlotte Observer,* p7
6. Quinn, Frank; (1959, October 18). Speaking Frankly. *The Montana Standard,* p19
7. Rigby, Dick; (1961, July 18). Coliseum Authority Offer Hockey Team For $1 A Year. *The Charlotte News,* p17
8. Clarke, Liz; (1992, November 25). Hockey, soccer on the way to Charlotte. *The Charlotte Observer,* 1B
9. Laye, Leonard; (1993, June 3). Checkers on the Marks with coach. *The Charlotte Observer,* 1B
10. Mehrtens, Cliff; (1996, December 27). Checkers deal Richmond loss. *The Charlotte Observer,* 1B
11. Mehrtens, Cliff; (1997, April 6). Checkers done for season. *The Charlotte Observer,* 1H
12. Mehrtens, Cliff; (1998, May 2). Checkers lose coach to ECHL foe. *The Charlotte Observer,* 1B
13. Mehrtens, Cliff; (2000, January 14). Checkers call for a change. *The Charlotte Observer,* 1C

2. MARCHING INTO THE GATE CITY

1. Graff, Todd; (2003, November 14). The Original Gets His Night. *News & Record*. https://greensboro.com/the-original-gets-his-night-longtime-greensboro-standout-don-carter-will-be-honored-tonight-at/article_2c94f519-050c-52a4-961a-feb65704063d.html
2. Williams, Matt. (2004, May 27). City added to lawsuit by ex-coach. *News & Record*. https://greensboro.com/city-added-to-lawsuit-by-ex-coach-greensboro-aided-an-effort-by-the-generals-owner/article_732c5540-1e7c-5b5b-8c00cec4aa21a379.html

3. PARTY OF NINE IN THE TWIN CITY

1. Sink, Richard; (1977, January 4). Fill 'er Up, Coach. *The Charlotte Observer*, 5B
2. Scott, David; (1982, October 25). Carolinas Take Thunderbirds' Hockey Under Their Wings. *The Charlotte Observer*, 8A
3. Harrington, Matt; (2002, December 4). Minor-league hockey team to finish season in Winston-Salem. *Triad Business Journal*. https://www.bizjournals.com/triad/stories/2002/12/02/daily29.html

4. BLUE RIDGE BREAKAWAY

1. Mitchell County Historical Society; (2017, December 19). Spruce Pine was Hockey Town, USA. https://mitchellnchistory.org/2017/12/19/spruce-pine-hockeytown-usa-2/
2. Scott, David; (1984, February 12). Minor League Hockey, Bucks Find Home In Spruce Pine. *The Charlotte Observer*, 1D
3. Russo, Michael; (2018, May 2). Much-traveled NHL exec Rick Dudley comes full circle in return to North Carolina. *The Athletic*. https://the-athletic.com/ 339835/2018/05/02/much-traveled-nhl-exec-rick-dudley-comes-full-circle-in-return-to-north-carolina/
4. Hardin, Ed; (1992, April 11). Coliseum With 5,000 Seats Sits Empty Now In Spruce Pine. News & Record. https:// greensboro.com/coli-

seum-with-seats-sits-empty-now-in-spruce-pine-hockey/article_a2b-b3553-53a4-5b67-9914-fe931a1253f6.html

5. Coughlin, Sean; (1998, August 19). Smoke sign (another) Gretzky. *Asheville Citizen-Times*, C1

6. Jarrett, Keith; (2000, April 14). Second-season report: Still smoking. *Asheville Citizen-Times*, E1

7. Richardson, Sandee; Kevin Carter; (1999, October 19); Canceled game may cost Smoke $100,000. *Asheville Citizen-Times*, A1

8. Jarrett, Keith; (2005, May 12). Civic Center profits from Aces lease. *Asheville Citizen-Times*, A1

5. CAPITAL INCURSION

1. Fun While It Lasted; (2011). Interview with Miles Wolff. https://fun-whileitlasted.net/wp-content/uploads/2020/01/November-2011-Miles-Wolff-Interview.pdf

2. Mehrtens, Cliff. (1997, May 8). ECHL's IceCaps waiting to move. *The Charlotte Observer*, 2B

3. Alexander, C., Eisley, M., Williams, B. (1996, December 5). Rift leaves Raleigh's NHL bid in doubt. *The News & Observer*, 1A

4. Williams, Bob. (1996, December 5). New tenants sought, but arena still a go. *The News & Observer*, 24A

6. FLINGING FISTS IN FAYETTEVILLE

1. Bednard, Shawn. (2018, December 20). Fayetteville's Surprising Historical Impact On Southern Hockey. *Bus League Hockey*. https://www.busleaguehockey.com/2018/12/20/fayettevilles-surprising-historical-impact-on-southern-hockey/

2. Pope, Thomas. (2017, April 6). Fayetteville FireAntz sold to ownership group run by former Fort Bragg soldier. *The Fayetteville Observer*. https://www.fayobserver.com/sports/20170406/fayetteville-fireantz-sold-to-ownership-group-run-by-former-fort-bragg-soldier

7. LANDFALL

1. Michaux, Scott. (1997, September 24). 'Canes Still High On the Hog. *Greensboro News & Record.* https://greensboro.com/canes-still-high-on-the-hog/article_074cf174-ce9d-5cc0-9333-68ffd1b45554.html

2. Droschak, David. (1997, November 5). Dispatcher call says Burke beat his wife before. *AP.* https://apnews.com/article/28d32fc5586566aaf258994a840e410c

3. Russo, Michael. (1998, February 22). Wake of Hurricane Sergei. *South Florida Sun-Sentinel.* https://www.sun-sentinel.com/news/fl-xpm-1998-02-22-9802210180-story.html

4. Callahan, Gerry. (1997, October 27). Natural Disaster. *Sports Illustrated.* https://vault.si.com/vault/1997/10/27/natural-disaster-the-hurricanes-have-stormed-into-north-carolina-but-they-havent-blown-anyone-away

5. CBS News. (1998, July 12). Francis Signs With Hurricanes. https://www.cbsnews.com/news/francis-signs-with-hurricanes/

6. Associated Press. (1998, September 10). Arturs Irbe Signs With Hurricanes. https://apnews.com/article/c9f4cf5e60dd6e43e2123a0f38ee69af

7. News & Record. (1998, December 29). CANES GET CHICAGO'S COFFEY IN TRADE\ THE VETERAN DEFENSEMAN ARRIVES JUST IN TIME FOR A CRUCIAL STRETCH OF SOUTHEAST DIVISION GAMES. https://greensboro.com/canes-get-chicagos-coffey-in-trade-the-veteran-defenseman-arrives-just-in-time-for-a/article_686bdfe5-2665-5c88-a97b-2bb418e4415c.html

8. Graff, Todd. (1999, May 4). OFFICER: ALCOHOL INVOLVED IN ACCIDENT\ STEVE CHIASSON'S BLOOD-ALCOHOL LEVEL AT THE TIME OF HIS FATAL CAR ACCIDENT WILL NOT BE KNOWN FOR TWO TO THREE WEEKS. https://greensboro.com/officer-alcohol-involved-in-accident-steve-chiassons-blood-alcohol-level-at-the-time-of-his/article_8e1b58c1-0ffa-5b87-b1f1-64f5e4fdb8a8.html

9. Associated Press. (1999, December 31). Primeau remains holdout with no deal. https://www.espn.com/nhl/news/1999/1230/259962.html

10. Droschak, David. (2002, January 15). Carolina Trades Ozolinsh to Florida. Associated Press. https://www.mrt.com/news/article/Carolina-Trades-Ozolinsh-to-Florida-7741121.php

11. Associated Press. (2001, November 11). Marchment Is Suspended. https://www.nytimes.com/2001/11/11/sports/hockey-marchment-is-suspended.html

12. SI Staff (2008, December 3). Hurricanes fire coach Laviolette. Sports Illustrated. https://www.si.com/nhl/2008/12/03/laviolette-fired

13. Associated Press (2009, May 12). Walker fined for punching Ward. ESPN. https://www.espn.com/nhl/playoffs/2009/news?id=4158572

14. Gold, Adam (2017, January 29). Karmanos willing to sell Hurricanes, but doesn't have to. WRAL Sports Fan. https://www.wralsportsfan.com/it-s-time-for-peter-karmanos-to-sell-the-hurricanes/16481894

ABOUT THE AUTHOR

Jeb Bohn is an author primarily known for his work in the suspense genre, though he also has works published in horror and non-fiction. With his full-length debut, Bermuda, he introduced readers to the world of cynical journalist Herman Ingram and won them over with his mix of suspense, thrills, and humor. He continued the series in 2020 with the release of two titles: The Hangman's Soliloquy and The Devil's Backyard.

When he's not writing, Jeb enjoys spending time with his family and taking long, aimless drives. He's a lifelong hockey fan.

ALSO BY JEB BOHN

Kill The Messenger

The Hangman's Soliloquy

The Devil's Backyard

Random Synapse Misfire, Vol. One

Random Synapse Misfire, Vol. Two

Strange Skies

The Last Cigarette

Made in the USA
Coppell, TX
14 November 2022